THE OTHER SIDE

A Lifeline of Hope to
Those on the Shore of Despair

ERICA HARMS

WESTBOW
PRESS®
A DIVISION OF THOMAS NELSON
& ZONDERVAN

WestBow Press books may be ordered through booksellers or by contacting:

WestBow Press
A Division of Thomas Nelson & Zondervan
1663 Liberty Drive
Bloomington, IN 47403
www.westbowpress.com
1 (866) 928-1240

THE HOLY BIBLE, NEW INTERNATIONAL VERSION®, NIV® Copyright © 1973, 1978, 1984, 2011 by Biblica, Inc.® Used by permission. All rights reserved worldwide.

ISBN: 978-1-9736-5195-6 (sc)
ISBN: 978-1-9736-5194-9 (hc)
ISBN: 978-1-9736-5196-3 (e)

Library of Congress Control Number: 2019900737

Print information available on the last page.

WestBow Press rev. date: 01/29/2019

What Readers are Saying about *The Other Side*

In her book, *The Other Side*, Erica Harms shares on such a transparent level her own story out of despair. She doesn't sugarcoat the hard reality that healing from trauma can be brutally painful but does offer hope and practical suggestions in the midst of it all. Page after page, Erica points to Jesus as the source of healing and redemption. Whether you've experienced the loss of a loved one, found yourself the survivor of abuse, or faced grief and heartache from a myriad of other circumstances, Erica's raw testimony is the encouragement you need to face the storm with courage.

-Ronda Brown, Trauma Informed Therapist

This book is unique because it has an extremely specific goal, helping trauma survivors find hope and healing in Jesus, yet is absolutely universal. It doesn't matter whether trauma occurs at the hands of other people, disease or circumstance. When we are going through it, we need messages from the other side. We need other survivors to remind us that one day at a time is a victory in and of itself. Part of the human condition is learning how to deal with disappointment and broken dreams. Erica reminds us that we are not alone and provides the example of how to lean in to a loving Father.

-Meredith Joy, Singer/Songwriter
at www.meredithjoymusic.com

The Other Side is a splendid offering of survival shared in a spirit of courage and transparency. Erica's steadfast expression of faith through seasons of turmoil is both refreshing and inspiring as she so eloquently writes from a once shattered yet mended heart. Each page offers encouragement for healing and the assurance of hope.

-Melanie C. Milton, Children's Author

To Jackie

Whose steadfast courage to walk a road with
me from total despair to the other side showed
me a picture of the beauty of the Gospel.

Contents

Acknowledgements

When I first stood on the shore of despair and the weight of this world came crashing in around me, I did not think I would ever write a book about my experiences. But the lessons I learned during the most difficult days are too valuable not to share. Writing a book about the story of my life has been a surreal process, but it is not primarily a story about me. Instead, it is a record of how God intervened during my traumatic experiences. Often, it was by bringing people into my life during such crucial times to minister to me in my darkest hour.

I'm forever indebted to Grace Thornton for your editorial help, keen insight, and ongoing support in bringing my story to life. I knew the moment you introduced me to the Delta during our Mississippi College days that we would be lifelong friends. I learned so much from you journalistically during our late-night adventures to frantically meet deadlines in the basement dungeon of the newspaper lab. Write on, friend! May your story inspire many.

To Meredith Duke, I will forever be grateful to the Lord for bringing us together when we both needed it most. Thank you for feeling the holy weight of this project and cheering me along as it came to fruition. I am inspired by the intensity of your compassion for others. You have a true gift for words, and I pray God uses it immensely as you minister to others through song.

Every once in a while, God sends that rare gift of an immediate connection to someone who becomes an instant heart friend. Ronda Brown, what did I do to deserve you? Some people go their whole life without finding their safe person, and I'm glad I'm not one of them. You are Pooh when this Piglet is trembling in fear. You make me brave. Personally and professionally, thank you for stepping in at my lowest and choosing just to be present. You have had every right to judge me but never once have. Your unconditional positive regard has gotten me through many days.

Jackie, my Paul. Where do I begin? Incessantly, you have pointed me to Jesus. We have both prayed that God would help me forget certain painful details of my story while leaving enough to help other people. As we've reminisced about experiences shared in this book, it's almost wildly obvious that God has answered those prayers. Thank you for believing for me when I couldn't. I am indebted to you for the quiet back bedroom you provided while I crammed for the GRE, retreated to when I hit rock bottom, and found courage in to fly to the other side of the world. I am even more indebted to you for the countless hours of walking and talking you sacrificed to direct me to the One who could lead me to the other side. Oh, and I would never have finished grad school without you!

Likewise, thank you to Teddy Bear Ray for sharing your wife and home. You have loved me as your own and protected me when I needed it most. Keep that quiet grin of yours.

I am especially grateful to my parents who have supported me in every sense. I always knew that you believed in me and wanted the best for me. You taught me to dream big and love deeply. My childhood was the foundation of faith, hope, and love that carried me into adulthood. Mom and Dad, you are proof that you can do everything right and still not be able to protect your child from everything. I'm confident that if you had known pieces of my story as they were unraveling that you would have dropped everything to rescue me. Thank you for your selfless love, care, and sacrifice that shaped my life. I love you dearly.

To Maelynn, this momma of yours sometimes lies awake at night worrying about the world and how you'll grow up here. There are these moments when I want to lock the doors and all the evil out and try my best to protect you from everything wicked and wild but have learned in my own journey that is not possible. Things are broken here, and there are some things I need to tell you to keep you soul-safe. I want the light in your heart to stay on when the world around you gets dark. There's a God who is good, who does love you and who's got this whole world in His hands. *But there will be days when it won't feel that way.* You'll look around and sit numb from the seeming pointlessness of it all and grasp for answers. Keep praying to the God I've told you about because when we pray, we reach out and grab hold of Someone who sees and hears, and therein lies our hope. There will be aching nights when you will struggle along, feeling around in the dark, searching for some notion of grace in this fallen world. And I want you to hear me—God is here. Right here. And when you run hard after Him, determined to find Him with a little speck of faith, He will show up. I love you to the moon and back. He loves you even more.

Most of all, I thank Jesus Christ, for without You is only a sea of despair. I cannot imagine going through life one single day without the hope that only You can give.

MY PRAYER

A blank page—so very long, so very white, so very intimidating,
Waiting to hold adventurous stories and thought-provoking challenges.
My mind is full of single ideas, waiting to collaborate for a final product.

I want the creativity to flow, letting my mind paint a picture with words,
Then allowing my fingers to dance across the page until the music stops.
I want these pages to leave the reader with innovative thoughts and
hope.

But I have only the brain and the fingers; the message comes from You.
So I hold up my blank page for the very Author of insight to fill.
Should You choose to share a message today, my fingers are available.

Preface

When I first felt like the Lord might be asking me to write this book, I cringed. I knew that to put my experiences into words might mean having to relive the pain associated with them all over again. But time and time again, I sensed that God wanted to use my story to speak hope into the lives of those who find themselves living in utter despair. It became all too common to hear, "Have you ever thought about writing a book?" until I knew with confidence that God indeed wanted me to pen the story of His work in my life. Only by sharing the ugly and painful details of my narrative do I believe I can give God all the credit He deserves for leading me to the other side. Whether you are a survivor of abuse or grieving the loss of broken dreams or shattered in a thousand pieces from betrayal, I'm here to tell you that there is hope because of our faithful God. There is a Redeemer who specializes in taking broken pieces and making stunning mosaics. We have a Defender who sees, who cares, and who is intimately acquainted with our suffering. You may be on the shore of despair now, but there is another side, and you're going to make it there!

-Erica

Introduction

Life stopped in the blink of an eye. One moment I was breathing and the next the air had been knocked right out of my lungs. There weren't enough tissues to wipe the tears away, not enough calm sensations to stop the trembling. I pulled the covers back over my head hoping to drown out the despair that was quickly burying me alive. I didn't know it was possible to feel that much agony, that much rage, that much grief and still live to tell about it.

I know what it's like to walk through the dark valley of despair. There were days when I gave up the desire to live, hours when I fought just to breathe in and out, days when I never stopped trembling, and moments when I lost all sight of hope. But from the other side, I am a living testimony of the Lord's redemptive hand at work. Healing is not a far-fetched dream; it's a promise.

Let me start by saying that if you're reading this thinking that I have all the answers and have it all together, you are grossly mistaken. On the contrary, I still struggle. I'm still fighting my own battles daily. I am a fellow struggler. I do not write as one who wants to fool you into thinking I am something that I'm not. Nope, I'm just a broken person like you trying to navigate this one shot at life. My goal in writing, rather, is to prove to you that you are not alone. Your pain is not isolated. Your feelings are valid.

Having experienced firsthand the depth of evil on earth, I don't do clichés. Quite frankly, I'm repulsed by them. While I know that good-hearted people speak them with the best of intentions, I cannot stomach them. When you've been cut to the core and the blood of traumatic experiences trickles down every fiber of your being, you don't need cliché; you need real. You need raw. You need to know that someone out there understands the ache that you cannot possibly find words to explain.

There was a time when I wondered if I'd ever be free. I'm not talking about freedom that comes from salvation. I grew up in the church. I know and believe deeply that Jesus came in order that we might have life and have it more abundantly, but I also know that you cannot have abundant life without being free. And if I were honest, I would have to say that I was anything but free. I was in chains. I was hurt. I was broken. I was confused. I was angry. I was in total despair.

Some of you can relate to that because you know what it looks like when your world falls apart. This book is written to those of you experiencing some of life's greatest suffering, regardless of where that suffering stemmed from. These vignettes from my own story are written for those of you asking, "Will I ever get through *this?*" Whatever your "this" is, there is hope. I promise.

I also write because at one point I couldn't. Somewhere along the way, in the midst of my deepest turmoil, I lost my voice. I was forced into silence, holding the bitter pain inside. Abuse silences us. Just the thought of telling my story was horrific because if I said it out loud, that would make it real. As long as it wasn't discussed, I still had hope that maybe it didn't really happen. I had fought for so long to forget the thoughts and feelings associated with sexual abuse. And yet, the fight to find words for my experience was perhaps the greatest step in my healing process. When I found someone safe I could confide in who helped to affirm the truth to me when I could not hold onto it myself, I found healing. To be stripped of our voice is painful. But to speak is equally painful because the telling makes our stories real.

When trauma happens, and we are overcome with fear, the neurotransmitters in our brains get stuck. Imagine a room where black filing cabinets line each wall. God wired our brains to constantly be processing information and storing it in its proper place. When trauma occurs, however, our brain gets stuck and does not know where to file details related to that experience. It just sits untouched, sometimes for years. But because it has not been filed properly, fear keeps showing up when we least expect it. Triggers arise in the form of sounds, smells, memories, images, and thoughts that can halt all forward progress and take us right back to the very experience we are trying to run from. The past enters the present over and over again until our brains can properly process and find words and meaning to what happened.

I now have a narrative for the chaos I once could not make sense of. I won't lie; telling my story was just as painful as the abuse itself. However, it was in sharing my story—over and over again—that I found healing. It's in sharing my story now that I continue to find healing. I found words for that which once had no words. It is now filed properly as a piece of my history that has affected who I am today but does not define me nor does it overwhelm me as it once did. I experienced the dark shadows of heartache and watched the light slowly emerge in those places I never wanted to revisit. I write now for those of you who are fighting to find words for your own experience.

Finally, I write because God's word is clear that as believers, we are supposed to battle sin and its effects head-on. We cannot ignore the reality of the fallen world in which we live. Some suffering is caused by things far out of our control—the death of a loved one, a miscarriage, a natural disaster, a terminal diagnosis. Some suffering, however, is the result of sin. The truth is that we are to stand in the gap for those who are both trapped in sin (Galatians 6:1) and suffering as a result of the sins of others (Galatians 6:2).

Just before sitting down to begin writing this book, I was watching the evening news. The top story for the day was about a man arrested for numerous counts of rape. The news anchor shared how one girl's courage to come forward with the reality of what happened to her opened the door for several others to do the same. My prayer is that the pages of this book might be like the voice of that child who paved a way for hard reality to be confronted. Keep in mind that there is a much greater picture than what our eyes can see. "Our struggle is not against flesh and blood, but against the rulers, against the authorities, against the powers of this dark world and against the spiritual forces of evil in the heavenly realms" (Ephesians 6:12).

In the spirit of total transparency, the act of writing this book has been a battle. There have been multiple moments when I have sat down to write and thought, "Do I really have a message to share?" I have fought nightmares and flashbacks and a myriad of other obstacles I hoped I'd never have to stare at again. On one of my most difficult evenings of writing, a precious friend and fellow therapist sent me a simple message that read "Jeremiah 30:2." I opened the Word to find, "This is what the Lord, the God of Israel, says: 'Write in a book all the words I have spoken to you.'" In that moment, I knew. I knew that while I was trembling in fear, I had to take a step of obedience in hopes that something I have learned on my journey would help someone else. I knew that I could have faith and fear simultaneously as long as I let faith lead.

So to those of you in the midst of enormous suffering and those of you who are watching one you love go through suffering, take heart. In order to experience joy, you will have to deal with sorrow. In order to experience hope, you will have to contend with despair. The way out is to deal with the very things that you want to run and hide from, but the truth is that you will come out on the other side. "Even though I walk *through* the darkest valley, I will fear no evil, for You are with me" (Psalm 23:4a). Don't miss it! Through—from one side to the other. There is another side and a God who will take you by the hand and lead you to it. Through the valley, yes, but to the other side.

PART ONE

DESOLATION:
THE SUDDEN
SHATTERING INTO
A MILLION PIECES

1

Am I Going to Make It?

For me, the breaking point happened late one night on a kitchen floor. I was staying with a precious couple who had taken me in as their own when I was an out-of-state college student in their college town. I had hit rock bottom. I was beyond terrified, beyond trapped, beyond shattered. My apartment had just been robbed and aware of the pitiful shape I was already in, they opened their home to me. She was washing the last of the dinner dishes in the kitchen sink when I peered my head around the corner, tears streaming down my face. I wasn't one to cry, and she knew it. The pain on the inside had finally surfaced when the tears had begun a couple of weeks earlier and hadn't stopped. Neither had the trembling. I was physically, mentally and emotionally depleted.

"I need to hear you say one more time that there is another side," I whispered to her.

She turned toward me with alligator tears in her own eyes. "Sit down," she replied as she dried her hands on a towel and plopped down on the floor between the sink and the stove. She took my hands in hers, cried right along with me, and promised me that there is another side.

That was the threshold for me, the point in which everything in me was screaming, "Am I going to make it through this?" This book is written for those of you wondering the same thing, those of you doubting if you can make it through, those of you who feel like taking one more step or one more breath may be too difficult to handle. You're not alone.

In my line of work as a counselor, I talk to people every day who are suffering. I see firsthand the effects of evil in this world and the ugliness of humanity. I work among the broken. They are asking, "When will these dark days be over?" They are questioning, "What did I do to deserve this?" They are saying, "I have never experienced a time as dark as this before. I don't see the Lord in this. I don't see how this is loving, how this is for my good, how there is hope and joy in *this*." They are wondering, "Why has He forsaken me?" Maybe you can relate. Those lines certainly came out of my mouth during my dimmest hours.

I will tell you that reading this book will be difficult. You have taken a brave step to even open the cover. There is something compelling about the other side because it means there is hope of authentic healing. But there is also something revolting about bringing to light the very parts of our existence that lived in darkness for so long. You will try to convince yourself that your pain happened too long ago to matter now. You will be tempted to minimize, deny, and hide. You will tell yourself, "It's no big deal," and perhaps even to "get over it." You will feel crazy for dealing with the emotions that well up within you. Do me a favor? Show yourself some grace as you move through these pages. Read at a slow pace if that's what you need. You will feel rage, resentment, bitterness, confusion, relief, and hurt. And you will be normal.

Since this book is written about how God wants to lead us to the other side of despair, it only makes sense that I first address my audience. This book is written to believers. We know that it is only by the power of God that we are able to reach the other side. If you do not have a personal relationship with Jesus Christ, you will never fully comprehend what God is doing in your life. You will never know the abundant life that God longs for us to have. If you are not a Christian, you need to know that God loves you and wants nothing more than to help you reach the other side. Perhaps you are in a place of total despair; everything around you is dark and you feel like your world is caving in. Have you ever been in a pitch-black room? I mean so black that you can't see your hand in front of your face? When even the smallest light is turned on, what was once hidden is suddenly illuminated. In John 8:12, Jesus refers to Himself as the Light of the World. If you are living in darkness, you are separated from God, and that is the darkest place to be. It's void, lonely, and hopeless. My prayer for you is that you embrace the Light of the World, even if all you can see right now is one tiny hint of Light.

The Bible says that every single person has sinned and fallen short of the glory of God (Romans 3:23) and that the wages of our sin is death (Romans 6:23). Knowing that we have all sinned, Jesus came to earth and lived a perfect life, willingly gave His life as a payment for our sin and was raised from the dead three days later. When He came back to life, He appeared before groups of people. In John chapter 20, there is a story about a man named Thomas, who was one of those people. He couldn't believe his eyes. Do you blame him? This man who died and was buried just days earlier was standing right in front of him. Thomas doubted that it was in fact Jesus. In verse 27, Jesus showed Thomas His scars, and instantly Thomas believed. I'm fascinated by this! In this passage, *Jesus used His scars to reveal His identity.* My scars— my trauma, my wounds, the signs of what I have experienced— reveal my identity too. They are a part of my story that scream, "Look what she has overcome!"

Think about a scar. It represents a past hurt or wound. Jesus was wounded for all of the garbage we once carried. The disciples knew the scars proved Jesus was in fact their risen Lord. Three times in this passage, Jesus tells His disciples, "Peace be with you." He can offer this peace to the disciples only because of the very scars He is showing them. Because He died a physical death on the cross and because God raised Him from the dead, He can offer new life and peace. Romans 10:9 says, "If you declare with your mouth, 'Jesus is Lord,' and believe in your heart that God raised Him from the dead, you will be saved." This peace is not just for the twelve men in the passage. It is for you, too. He is also *your* risen Lord. His scars are also for *you*. Jesus is intimately acquainted with grief and heartache. He understands your pain. He knows your hurt. He wants you to know Him, so that together, He can lead you to the other side.

To those of you who are Christians, let me direct you to the first chapter of 1 Peter. Peter is writing to the various churches suffering as a result of religious persecution. While your particular suffering may be for entirely different circumstances, he is writing nonetheless to the broken-hearted. His audience is asking "Are we going to make it?" In its context, let me highlight verse 5 for a moment:

> Praise be to the God and Father of our Lord Jesus Christ! In His great mercy He has given us new birth into a living hope through the resurrection of Jesus Christ from the dead, and into an inheritance that can never perish, spoil or fade. This inheritance is kept in heaven for you, *who through faith are shielded by God's power* until the coming of the salvation that is ready to be revealed in the last time. In all this you greatly

rejoice, though now for a little while you may have had
to suffer grief in all kinds of trials. These have come so
that the proven genuineness of your faith—of greater
worth than gold, which perishes even though refined
by fire—may result in praise, glory and honor when
Jesus Christ is revealed. (1 Peter 1:3-7)

If the outcome on the other side enables us to think like Peter,
we'll have a voice that can never be taken from us. Even when
it feels like we are being attacked on every side, we are shielded
by God's power. The word "shielded" in this verse is the same
word used in Philippians 4:7 when Paul writes that "the peace
of God will guard our hearts and minds in Christ Jesus." There
is comfort in knowing that the Lord will protect us because we
are His children. It's important to know that Peter is not saying
that God will guard believers by exempting them from pain or
suffering. Oh how many times I have wished that were the case!
Instead, he is saying that God will guard them from that which
will cause them to fall away from their faith. Ephesians 6:16 tells us
that it is our faith that extinguishes the flaming arrows of the evil
one. It is our faith—our faith in One who sees the big picture—
that brings God's power in to fight for us.

God is at work running interference on our behalf. Hold on
tightly. When you feel the pressure from the battle field, fight to
believe that God is charging the enemy lines in front of you. Fight
what you *know* to be true rather than what you *feel* is true. Can't
you just hear Peter shouting toward the battle lines: "Hold on!
This trial is just showing off your faith! You're gonna make it!"

"You will feel rage, resentment, bitterness, confusion, relief, and hurt. And you will be normal."

2

The Truth Comes Out

My story is not about a particular situation or incident. It's about tragedy turned to hope and deep sorrow turned to joy. It's about Someone greater than all our circumstances. It's about victory when all I could smell was ashes. Perhaps it's not always the "how" or the "what" that caused the pain that is important. The commonality is that it's all pain, and we belong to a God who delivers and heals. With that in mind, I believe it is much more beneficial for me to share the effects of my suffering rather than the details of its cause.

Therapists commonly say that "it will get worse before it gets better" when you really begin to unpack the mound of emotions you are feeling as you go through the grieving process. It's true. It's like a rubber band ball. When you identify one emotion, you discover that it's tied to another and another and another. The more you explore, the more chaotic life seems and the more out of control you feel. The bravest thing I have ever done is say the words "I've been sexually abused" for the first time, because it meant I would have to deal with what was to follow. I'll never forget the first time I said those words. I was with my mentor friend one afternoon in a quaint little coffee shop. She asked the right questions, and I didn't have the courage to look her in the eyes and lie, so she got truthful answers. For the next three hours, I cried and trembled uncontrollably. The room spun and I could not tell which way was up and which way was down. It was the first tears I'd cried in years. I had been terrified to let a single tear fall out of fear that I wouldn't be able to stop crying once I started. My fear was valid but was matched by the tears spilling from her own eyes. I'm sure it was quite a sight as people passed by us on that chocolate brown couch at the front of the coffee shop to grab their afternoon lattes! As those first tears welled up in my eyes, it was a moment of panic and a moment of triumph. I was free from the secret, and I was found out.

I learned more about grace that afternoon than the rest of my life combined. I can remember her saying through her own tears, "I've never been more honored than I am right now that you would share this with me." I didn't understand why, of all things, honor was something she was feeling, but the look on her face told me I could believe her. She knew. She knew my secret. She knew what I had fought for so long to hide. Like a flood, I was relieved and terrified at the same time. I was hopeful and in despair. My mind knew, "It's not your fault." It knew, "Your power and voice were taken from you." But I couldn't believe any of that with my heart at that time.

It was a strange feeling leaving the coffee shop that day. I felt such relief from having told her and was thankful she was brave enough to ask the hard questions, but I was utterly gripped with fear. I sat in my car for what seemed like an eternity just trying to remember how to turn it on. I was indeed flooded with emotions, in the center of the rubber band ball without seeing a way out. Many of the days that followed are a blur. I couldn't speak, couldn't eat, and couldn't sleep. I didn't want to go to work, didn't want to get out of bed, and certainly didn't want to be around people. When I was, I remained silent. I wish that I could tell you I hit my knees in prayer and opened God's word to find some reassurance, but the truth is that I couldn't focus my mind to do either of those things. I was fighting just to function. Sometimes you are so mentally and emotionally exhausted that it is tough to even think. To inhale and then to exhale is victory. Just being is hard enough.

I was numb. I tried not to think because it didn't lead anywhere good, but when I did, I felt like I was going absolutely crazy. I would physically tremble throughout the day. I would find myself zoned out, remembering things and places and details, smells and sights and sounds. I asked myself, "Did that really happen?" a thousand times. The more I wrestled with that question, the more memories came and the more I crumbled. I suddenly became terrified of having my back to anyone. I would jump if someone approached me from behind or if I heard a noise I wasn't expecting. I trusted no one. I was absolutely paralyzed by fear.

I can remember one Sunday morning that I was sitting next to my friend in church. I found myself engulfed in a flashback when I felt her lean up against my arm to pull my mind back to the present. My eyes had glazed as my mind wandered back to the most horrendous memories— until I heard my name. "Erica. Erica, look around you. You're sitting in the sanctuary at church. You are next to me. You are safe." I would blink back to the present, take a long look around, and breathe a sigh of relief.

The grief was so overwhelming that it became a constant fight to draw a line between the past and the present. I would go to bed at night only to wake up to one nightmare after another. It was not until after I had voiced my story that first time that the memories that I had fought so hard to forget began to haunt me, and boy did they torment me!

One of the many things that my mentor encouraged me to do

during this critical time was to try to journal, something that I used to be so faithful to do but had not done since the abuse started. I had attempted so many times to put my feelings on paper, but more often than not, I ended up putting my pen down before one word was ever written on the page, too overwhelmed to continue. I can remember how proud I felt those few times I was able to find words for my emotions. I would give myself permission to stop if necessary. I gave myself permission to write, erase, rewrite, ramble, whatever it took to put something—anything—on paper. Below is an excerpt from my journal on one of the nights I was successful in finding words.

> *My mind is racing, legs trembling. Mind too busy to sleep. Legs too wobbly to make it up the stairs. I have said several times that I hate myself. I think the wording of that is not accurate. Every time I say those words, a battle rages, knowing that what God created was good. God created me and was pleased. It's not that I hate myself. I hate feeling helpless. I hate feeling powerless. I hate feeling defeated. Should I have run? Of course! Should I have screamed, hit, fought, told? Of course! But I couldn't. I was frozen. I hate that I was frozen. Right or wrong, I blame myself for being frozen. That's what I hate. Will it benefit me to relive it all? More than likely. No way to remain in denial in doing that, and admitting it happened and working through it is how you get to a healing place. But I want to do all that work in a safe environment. I need to know when to pull out and when to keep going, and I'm just not sure I can do that on my own right now. It's all too overwhelming.*

I sent that journal entry to my friend. A portion of her response to me said, "I am really proud of you. I love you. I believe in you. God is always at work in your life. This will work for good, perhaps beyond that which you'll ever know." I have held on to that e-mail because it spoke words of life to me. She knew my deepest pain and loved me all the more because of it. And ... she saw the other side when I could not. She believed for me. And now today, I am here believing for you.

*"I was free from the secret,
and I was found out."*

3

Rock Bottom

I was in Birmingham for a work conference when I got the phone call. It was my roommate. "Erica, did you leave your bedroom light on?" That was the first thing she said, and it went downhill from there. She gasped, noticing a foot print by the door handle. I heard her fumble for her keys as she got back in her car. We had been robbed. It did not take the police long to arrive, and they entered first while she was on the phone with me. "Your guitar is gone, and my computer is gone off the couch." Then the scream. The front door had been kicked in, and the sight obviously had her shaken. She talked me through her going upstairs, turning the corner, and seeing her bedroom completely demolished. I remained on the other end calm, cool, and collected—long enough to hang up the phone. I was standing inside a store when all of this was taking place. I put down the few items I had intended to purchase and went out to my car. After I hung up the phone, the tears started streaming. The anger began to surface. I remember shouting, "I've been violated again!" at the top of my lungs and beating the steering wheel uncontrollably. It had only been a couple of weeks since that afternoon in the coffee shop with my friend. Since then, the only safe place had been my home. Now that was taken from me.

I sat in my car for quite some time. The hotel where I was staying was not far up the road, but I was not sure I could make it there. If I were honest, I was not sure I wanted to make it there. My world felt so out of control and fear had absolutely overwhelmed me. I had a good friend living in Birmingham at the time. I found enough sense to pick up the phone and call her. We agreed to meet at the hotel, and it was the accountability I needed to get there unharmed. I collapsed on the hotel floor, quivering and trying to catch my breath. She just wrapped a blanket around me and sat on the floor next to me. There were no magic words, or she would have spoken them, but her presence that night was God's gift to me. Soon after getting in my room, the telephone rang again. It was my mentor's husband from my apartment. His presence in my life had increased since the day I spent in the coffee shop with his wife. "I need you to stay put tonight. Don't try to drive back tonight." He and I both knew I had no business driving after such a shock, but he also knew I was stubborn enough to try. I promised him that I would stay put and call him when I got on the road in the morning. Then he handed the phone to his wife. She was in my bedroom, trying to pull out what she could before they boarded up the apartment for the night. I muttered the only thing I could find words to say.

"You know I just want to die, right?"

Her immediate response: "It's just more than you can handle right now, isn't it?"

It was such a calming, peace-filled voice in that horrific moment. I remember feeling guilty that I was talking with them on the phone while they were with my roommate at the apartment. She needed them in that moment. She was the one present who saw the destruction. And yet, while I'm thankful I was not the one who came home to it first, I believe I had the worst end of the situation. Have you ever noticed how our imagination can worsen any situation? Imagination can be a scary thing, and that's all I had to go on based on what I was being told over the phone.

I didn't sleep that night. My mind went in a thousand directions. The drive home was long. My mind was racing faster than my emotions could keep up with, and my body was aching from weeks of unrest. I drove straight to my safe people, and together with my roommate, we went to the apartment. When I first walked inside, I didn't move. I just stood in the living room for a little while. I didn't want to look around. Slowly I began to make my way around the apartment, making a mental inventory of what was missing, all the while crumbling on the inside. It was eerily quiet. My mentor followed close behind me, giving me space to go where I wanted to go but close enough to pick me up should I collapse.

My roommate and I spent the next four nights at their house. I jumped at every noise I heard, did not sleep, and fought to keep the littlest amount of food down. (I'm still thankful for banana popsicles!) My whole world seemed to have fallen apart in three weeks. I had never been one to struggle with depression or wanting to die before. I grew up in Mayberry, so to speak, with an incredible Christian family. I was active in church since I was in my mother's womb and would have been classified as a happy and healthy individual on every front. And I was. But this series of unexpected events took me lower than I had ever imagined was possible for me to go. I guess it was a pride thing. Was I so special that other Christians could battle with depression, but I couldn't? Was I so special that I should be exempt from this kind of suffering? Was I so special that it was okay for others to cry but I had to remain strong? No! A thousand times no. The truth is that I was a believer, and I wanted to die. I had surrendered my heart to Jesus but questioned why it was now in a thousand pieces. It was one of those four nights that I broke down on the kitchen floor and said, "I need to hear you say one more time that there is another side."

I wasn't alone in my feelings, and neither are you. The Bible talks of several people who wanted to end it all because of their afflictions. In Numbers 11, Moses was in despair because of the complaints of the Israelites whom he was leading. Leadership became more than he could handle, and he said, "I cannot carry all of these people by myself. The burden is too heavy for me. If this is how you are going to treat me, please go ahead and kill me" (vs. 14-15b). In the fourth chapter of Jonah, Jonah said, "Now, Lord, take away my life, for it is better for me to die than to live (vs. 3)." He repeated the same request to God on the next day. When Elijah got discouraged, he sat down under a tree and prayed, "I have had enough, Lord. Take my life; I am no better than my ancestors" (1 Kings 19:4b). In the midst of extreme physical pain, having lost several of his family members in an awful tragedy as well as his possessions, Job felt like giving up. He said, "I loathe my very life" (Job 10:1). These were men of great faith who wanted to die.

At the time, these men could not see past their pain. Their thinking was not right. I've been there. I love God's response to Elijah after he prayed to die: "Get up and eat" (1 Kings 19:5). It seems like a rather ironic response, but it was quite timely. God knew that Elijah was physically exhausted. When we are physically exhausted, we are mentally and emotionally exhausted as well. Elijah ate some bread, drank a jug of water, and went to sleep. Again an angel of the Lord woke him up and told him to eat, which he did. Scripture records that Elijah was strengthened as a result. Proper nourishment, hydration, and sleep are essential to the healing process. My friend knew that. When I could not think clearly, she did so for me, making sure those things became a priority. She sent me to bed. She put small amounts of food directly in my hands. Sleep. Eat. Drink.

It sounds so simple, but taking care of ourselves physically is the first step toward taking care of ourselves emotionally. That was a lesson I learned then that I would need years later when I'd hit rock bottom again.

"When we are physically
exhausted, we are mentally and
emotionally exhausted as well.

4

A Season of Rest

Some of my fondest memories come from the summer I spent hiking the Sawtooth Mountains in Idaho. I was part of a team of college students who led teenagers on lengthy hikes that tested their physical and mental endurance and ultimately provided them a worship experience with God free from the distractions of their normal lives. On one particular excursion, our team leader brought his young son along. The goal was to make an eleven-mile hike up to the peak on the first day, spend the night overlooking the most beautiful mountain view, and hike back out the next day. On the first day, we came to a briskly flowing creek, and the only way to cross it was to walk along a tree trunk that had fallen across it. This tree trunk was probably four feet above the water and twelve to fifteen feet in length. One by one, we climbed up on the tree trunk with our fifty-pound backpacks strapped to our back and slowly began to step forward. It was a test of mental focus and physical balance. Three members of the team had made it to the other side when our leader's son climbed up one side of the trunk. It was his turn. He made it to the very center of the tree before he slipped. He flailed his arms and frantically tried to regain balance but ultimately fell backwards into the water. The rushing water was fierce and forced him under the log. He was pinned between his still-strapped-on backpack and the log with his face under water. Instantaneously, his father threw his own backpack to the ground and jumped in after his son. It was a rescue unlike any I've ever seen before. He managed to loosen his son's backpack to get his face above water and then swam him to shore against the water's current. This child had taken in a lot of water, and we knew hypothermia could set in with mountain water. He and his father were noticeably shaken. We made an executive decision that day to stop hiking and set up camp right there at the water's edge. We didn't make it eleven miles that day. Instead, we built a fire and exchanged dry clothes. We cooked a warm meal and spent the rest of the day and night simply resting.

Sometimes events happen in life that force us to have to stop and rest. The sharing of my abuse was one of those events for me. I had completed a master's program in the field of counseling, but in that season of my life, I needed a rest from counseling others, and God provided that. I needed a period of time to heal myself, knowing that I could not give what I did not have. I pursued a career in an entirely different field for a while. I allowed myself time to process and grieve and rebuild what had been broken. For a couple of years, I rested and allowed God to do the healing work that only He can do.

I'd love to tell you exactly how I went from being unable to eat and sleep to truly living again. I wish there was a step-by-step process I could share of how to make sorrow disappear, but there's not. I took one day at a time, daily writing down at least three things I was thankful for that day. I stayed connected to a local body of believers who encouraged me when I was down. I sought counseling from an outside professional. I made it a point to turn on worship music whenever I could to drown out the lies in my head. I allowed myself to start trusting people again, and even got married. I posted Scripture verses throughout my house and on the dashboard of my car. I took care of myself physically and rested. I dug my heels in deep and declared, "Satan, you will not win." And slowly, over time, light began to emerge in the places that once held me captive. It was not a sudden change for me, but a slow shift. One day I woke up and realized that I felt peace, that my heart was calm, and that I looked forward to facing the day. My vision was clear, my thinking was positive, and my breathing was relaxed.

I thank God that He provides seasons of nourishment. He knows that we are frail humans who need rest for the journey. Perhaps that's why He tells us, "Come to Me, all you who are weary and burdened, and I will give you rest. Take My yoke upon you and learn from Me, for I am gentle and humble in heart, and you will find rest for your souls. For My yoke is easy and My burden is light." (Matthew 11:29).

That night as we camped by the water's edge, none of us wished we were at the top of the mountain looking out over the lights below. Instead, we were all just thankful to have crossed the hurdle of the log and be safe on the other side. Sometimes we find ourselves in a season of rest, neither standing on the mountaintop nor crumbling in the valley below. We can be tempted to feel bored or grow inpatient with what seems to be a lack of movement. It is critical in those middle times, to shift our perspective and recognize that God is allowing us to rest. Rest is not idleness; it is not a distraction. Rest, in every sense, is vital to our very existence.

Time does not heal all wounds. Time is not a healer; God is. But healing does take time, and what we do with that time matters. Time grows the seeds that are planted and fertilized.

In those times of calm, we can set up camp and rest in our Creator. He knows that the journey ahead is long and difficult and is giving us want we need for the task before we even know we need it.

"Time does not heal all wounds.
Time is not a healer; God is. But
healing does take time, and what
we do with that time matters."

5

Buried Alive

When the phone rang with news that my husband and I had been chosen as a match for a little boy in the foster system, the joy was unparalleled. We were going to provide him with a forever home, a family to unconditionally love him as he navigated his way through the effects of childhood trauma. We had been in the adoption process for over a year and had completed the grueling home study. We had done our share of fundraising. We had completed all the classes necessary to know what to expect when adopting a child from an abusive situation. We had agonized through the waiting process month after month. And the time was finally here! Until it wasn't.

The doctor knocked on the door and slowly made his way inside my exam room. "You're pregnant, Erica." I swallowed hard. How could this be? We had tried unsuccessfully for years to get pregnant. We had resigned ourselves to the fact that we would never have a child. We were eager to adopt one into our family to love as our own. We had prayed and sought the Lord's direction, and never once did we feel this was what would happen.

"Are you sure?" I asked the doctor, still trying to catch my breath.

I went home that day with my head spinning and some decisions to make. I broke the news to my husband and after much prayer and contemplation, we decided it best to halt the adoption process. That was a very difficult phone call to have to make. But in hindsight, God knew exactly what He was doing.

In the months to follow, I found myself in the biggest storm of my life. Early on in my marriage, clouds of distrust had surfaced. Those clouds grew increasingly darker. We had sought marital counseling years earlier, but the sin of this world kept wreaking havoc and rearing its ugly head until it ate away at the foundation of trust we had built. I found myself becoming more resentful and more fearful with each passing day until I knew something had to be done. I needed help for me.

For years, I hadn't told anyone the struggles we were facing. I thought I ought to have been strong enough to handle the growing fears. I should have been able to portray a beautiful picture of Christ with His bride to the world. I should have known how to better handle each difficult situation. I ought to have been stronger... wiser...better. I could go on, but the point is that Satan often works in the "should" and "ought" thoughts. When we hold on too tightly to these statements about ourselves, it almost always leaves us feeling guilty for not being able to meet our own expectations. And when we hold on to "should" statements too tightly about other people, it almost always imposes a set of expectations they can't live up to. I was dying a slow death on the inside by keeping silent, so I poured out my heart to Christian counsel.

I remember the day I took my wedding ring off. I twirled it around between my fingers remembering the beautiful proposal and promise of "'til death do us part." I remember the sunny November day that I stood before a crowd and made a promise to God and my husband. Broken dreams. Shattered expectations. Fragmented promises. I was six months pregnant with our first and only child when my marriage fell apart. My childhood fairytale dreams of getting married, having 2.5 kids, and growing old together were a crumpled mess on the floor.

As a counselor, I have now worked with dozens of divorced men and women who didn't throw their marriages away. Like me, they fought to the bitter end for their marriages until they realized they could either save their marriage or save their life. Their divorces forced them to wrestle with questions like, "How do I reconcile this with a good God?" "Why didn't God save my marriage?" "What does this say about me?" Like them, I had done everything I knew to do to fight for my marriage, and in the end it fell apart. When people say that divorce is like death, I understand why. Divorce is like being buried alive. I still had air in my lungs, but all I could see was darkness.

And sadly, one of the most difficult aspects of divorce to heal from for me was the response of a few believers within the walls of the church. I had been an active part of the same local body of believers for many years. I had deep rooted relationships with many people in that church. We shared meals together in each other's homes and spent holidays together. They were indeed my family. And yet, when my life crumbled, and news began to spread of my divorce, I was shocked at who chose to run out when what I needed most was people to run in.

"How can you just give up like that?" I can still hear the condemning voice on the other end of the phone. Thankfully, it's lost its sting now because I have fought it with the truth. After all these years, didn't she know me better than that? Didn't she know that I had done everything but quit? I was also told, "God hates divorce. If you love Him, you wouldn't get divorced." For starters, it takes two to get married and one to get divorced. But beyond that, don't you think that I know that God hates divorce? Everyone who's been divorced hates it too. No one stands on their wedding day and hopes to get divorced. No one joins into a union with someone else hoping to get ripped in two. God also hates lying, adultery, lust, greed, and every other sin people have ever committed. The verbal daggers came from those I'd wept with, laughed with, grown in the faith with, and worshipped alongside of for years, which is perhaps why they stung the most.

My marriage wasn't the only relationship I lost in divorce. Unfortunately, I had to part ways with others who had once been such close companions and sojourners in the faith. Every lost relationship felt like another piece of me dying. But in order to rise above the crashing waves, I had to silence any voice that contradicted the voice of the One who could calm the storm.

Now let me be clear on something. I, by no means, want to categorize an entire congregation as hurtful. There were many believers who held my hand and walked with me through the wilderness from that same body of believers. My point is simply that sometimes our greatest pain comes from the direction we least expect. I believe that Satan often uses other believers to do his dirty work.

The church is made up of sinners, and sinful people by nature hurt other people. Put a group of people together and life's bound to get messy, even (perhaps especially) within the walls of the church. But our enemy is not, nor ever has been, the person next to us on the pew. Satan hates God, and therefore hates God's church. His sole mission is to destroy it. He is not above using shameful strategies, including God's people, to tear us to shreds. He will twist words and twist meanings and instill hints of distrust and discord wherever there is room to do so. Wounds that come from the church are perhaps the deepest, most raw wounds to endure and can leave lifelong scars.

Why are religious people typically who are most astounded by mercy? We sweep our mess under the rug, hide our anger, conceal our doubts, and pretend that somehow it honors God for us to deny our frailty, the very thing that makes us human. Perhaps the people closest to God are those fighting for sobriety in recovery meetings, those who have walked inside the local pregnancy center, or those who have checked themselves into the psych ward. They're not dressed up trying to impress anyone. They have refused to pretend any longer. They are the ones who have felt the pain of rock bottom and know that no amount of pretending can bring about the healing for which they long for so desperately.

Do you know what I needed during that season of my life? I needed believers who said, "I may not understand everything you're going through, but I'm here for you." I needed people who left judgment at the door and came inside just to wrap their arms around me and give me hope when all I could do was cry. I needed people who didn't have a handful of magic words to make the pain disappear but who just showed up to be present with me in the pain. I needed friends who saw who the real enemy was and joined forces with me to fight him. And God, knowing this, provided.

"We sweep our mess under the rug,
hide our anger, conceal our doubts,
and pretend that somehow it honors
God for us to deny our frailty, the
very thing that makes us human."

6

Bulletproof Love

Fortunately, I had relocated to middle Tennessee just months prior to this, and my blood family was a rock for me during this time. My sister and her family live in Asia and the morning my husband left me, my parents had boarded an airplane headed to visit them. It was my brother and his wife who came over that night and wrapped their arms around me. Once again, I was in need of people encouraging me to eat, forcing me to sleep, and handling the very basics of functioning for me. I needed people reminding me to breathe. And this time, the little life growing inside of me was depending on me to do so. The first night my brother and sister-in-law stayed with me, they prayed over me, and one of the things I remember my brother saying was, "You're not damaged goods, Erica." I crumbled. It was the very words God knew I needed to hear. I felt used and abandoned yet again.

Those first few days are still a blur to me, but from them I do have a fond memory of yellow daffodils. At some point each day, my brother and his wife walked with me down the steep driveway, around a curve, and into an open field. Along the tree line grew hundreds of wild yellow daffodils. It was a beautiful Spring reminder of life in the midst of what felt like death. We would pick a fresh bouquet for the kitchen each day, and as we looked at those fresh flowers, my sister-in-law encouraged me to consider something positive that I had encountered that day. It was again encouragement to focus my mind on a higher realm.

I moved in with my parents just before my daughter was born and they helped me through all those sleepless nights and exhausting days of having a newborn once she arrived. They gave me strength until my own returned. My mother even placed a journal on the kitchen counter where we would record the various ways that we saw God provide and care tenderly for my heart during those days. Random bags of diapers would show up. Bills were suddenly paid off. Surprise baby showers were thrown. Unexpected phone calls came in the middle of the night to lift my spirits. Letters came in the mail to remind me that I wasn't alone. God's love for me during that battle was absolutely bulletproof. I had joined a new body of believers when I moved to Tennessee, and God began to establish deep friendships. I'd need these over the next several months of being a new mom and walking through the legal side of divorce.

I remember the unusually warm December day that I walked out of the courthouse as a divorced woman. I walked across the street to a local bakery and ordered a small chai latte and a white chocolate raspberry scone. I sat down at a high-top bistro table in the front corner that overlooked the quaint downtown. It appeared everyone else was going about life as usual. Christmas shoppers passed by the window with charming bags in their hands. Runners jogged the sidewalk listening to their headphones. Business men crossed the street from the parking garage headed to their workplaces. Yet my life had come to a crashing halt. I penned these words that day in my journal:

"Well, it's finally official. Five years plus one month of marriage. Ten excruciating months of divorce. Not really sure how I'm feeling right now. Relieved, disappointed, sad, happy, angry, crushed, broken, free ... just to name a few. It's a day of celebration. No, I don't celebrate a failed marriage. That's never what I would have chosen, but I celebrate a blank page, the official signature needed to begin again. I celebrate having survived. I celebrate relief. In some ways, I feel I failed. No one wins in divorce. Everyone loses. It's never what God intended, yet here I am. Thankfully, God has been speaking truth over me the past several months of my worth and value in Him. He doesn't reject me. He won't walk away. His love is not conditional. I've gained a lot of insight as I've navigated through this journey. And it's true: what doesn't kill you makes you stronger. I've learned who in my life is trustworthy and runs in when others run out. And I've certainly learned that my former union was worth it all to have those precious eyes and that sweet little grin staring me in the face. I am eternally grateful for friends and family who have taken me in and loved on me in the most practical ways. I am thankful for the Church and a God who is big enough to take a million shattered pieces and make something new and beautiful. Today I've closed one chapter and am about to begin the next. Is it over? No, it never will be fully. It's part of my story. The days/weeks/months/years ahead will have their fair share of tears and heartache related to this, but my personal restoration is underway, and for that I rejoice. So ... here's a toast to what lies ahead—whatever that may be. I can face uncertain days because my God is already there, working for my good and His glory, daily reminding me of who I am in Him. If God can transfigure the greatest evil into the greatest Gift, then He can turn this into a gift as well."

Healing is a process. True, lasting healing comes slowly. That can be exasperating, but it is what endures. I don't know about you, but I'm not interested in a counterfeit healing that comes for a little while and dissipates when the next crisis comes. I need a healing that endures. And lasting healing, though we may search for it in a variety of ways, comes only from one place. So, what do we do when God seemingly doesn't hear, doesn't respond, or doesn't remove the source of pain? We make assumptions that we aren't worthy of healing or that He doesn't really care about our suffering. Worse, we often conclude God has forgotten about us. Indeed, He has not. There is One who sees our suffering, knows our circumstances, feels our heartache, hears our cries, and restores what has been lost. Our hope is this: we know the Problem Solver, even if He chooses not to solve our problems. We know the Healer, even if He hasn't brought healing. We know the Redeemer, even if He hasn't brought redemption to our circumstances.

It's worth it to me to put in the hard work it takes for authentic healing to change my perspective and ultimately mend my broken heart. It is true that in great pain lies great strength. Just like mountains are formed from earthquakes and beautiful islands are formed from volcanoes, so our fortitude is formed out of crisis. Slowly, God began to shine light through the cracks of my brokenness. I'm convinced that the light of His presence is best seen against the canvass of darkness. As I sat there, feeling buried alive, the only place to look was up. And up is where I saw Him.

"I'm convinced that the light of His presence is best seen against the canvass of darkness."

PART TWO

RECONSTRUCTION: THE SLOW PROCESS OF BECOMING A MOSAIC

7

I Need Help

I've shared the highlights of my story, the traumatic situations that have impacted my life the most. By now, you may be reading this thinking, "I can't even relate to her story; mine is so different." Let me respond: pain is pain. Hurt is hurt. Trauma is trauma. If we were sitting face to face over a cup of coffee right now, you might share your story and I, too, would feel like I can't even relate to the horrors you've endured. But we can't minimize or deny our own experiences. No one gets to tell your story but you. No one gets to say how you feel but you. What you experienced is uniquely yours, but there are a few common threads in many of our stories. The God who led me to the other side is the same God who wants to lead you there as well. The God who told the wind and the waves to hush is the same God who helps us tell the lies in our head to hush. And the God who has redeemed my life from murky waters has shown me a few of the treasures along the way that I believe can also be beneficial for you as you stare at the other side.

It is hard for independent people like me to admit they need help. Have you noticed that the church is full of silent sufferers? I was one of them. Maybe you are too. There is a lie we believe that says that if our faith is strong, we should be able to get through whatever it is we are struggling with alone. The pews are full of Christians believing this lie. My friends, this ought not be! I have a newsflash for you: It's okay to not be okay. It's okay to need help. That is why we belong to a body of believers, a family of Christians who carry one another's burdens. That's what it means to have the strong helping the weak. When we choose to believe the lie that we can make it on our own, we are robbing the church of one of its fundamental God-ordained tasks. Jesus himself said that He did not come for the healthy, but for the sick (Mark 2:17). There are times in life when we are strong, times when we feel like we are coasting along without too many waves in life. Those are the times when 2 Corinthians 1:3-5 come alive. We are able to comfort those in trouble with the comfort we ourselves have received. Yet, there are times in our life when we are weak. There are times when, quite simply, we just need help. It is in those times that we must be vulnerable and admit our need for help. We cannot expect the church to help carry our burdens if they do not know our burdens exist.

1 Peter 1:6-7 says, "In this, you greatly rejoice even though you have had to suffer grief in all kinds of trials. These have come so that the proven genuineness of your faith—of greater worth than gold, which perishes even though refined by fire—may result in praise, glory and honor when Jesus Christ is revealed." Our faith does not determine the amount of suffering we will or will not endure. Our faith simply reminds us that we belong to a God who is big enough to see us out when we cannot see a way out. Our faith results in praise, glory, and honor to Jesus. He who began a good work will be faithful to complete it, and when He does, the world will see that our faith is genuine.

I remember so vividly the afternoon I was asked if I thought

I needed to go see a counselor. I didn't hesitate to answer, "Yes." "Would you go?" That second question was where I was stuck in my tracks. I knew I needed help, but it would require laying aside my pride to get it. I had received my master's in marriage and family therapy. I had seen clients for years. I carried hope for them when they could not carry it for themselves. I listened as they struggled to find words for their experiences. I cried when they cried. I laughed when they laughed. I watched God transform life after life in my presence. I journeyed with clients who were starting at rock bottom. And now, I was being asked if I would be willing to switch seats in the therapy room, to sit in the client's seat and open up to a counselor. Again, it was a matter of pride. Was it okay for others to need to seek me for counseling but not okay for me to need help? I knew the answer to that. Healers are in need of the same work as the broken. I made that hard phone call.

I began to see a godly counselor on a weekly basis, sometimes twice a week. I believe with all my heart that everyone can benefit from counseling. There is a preconceived notion that counseling is for "crazy people" and that nothing good can come from opening up to a complete stranger. Most people think that they will be looked down upon if they are known to attend counseling. The Bible has a lot to say about those who think they can make it on their own. It is referred to as independence, pride, and arrogance—all are sin. Proverbs 12:15 says, "The way of a fool seems right to him, but the wise listen to advice." Sometimes we all need an opportunity to gain self-awareness from someone on the outside not consumed by the chaos taking place on the inside of us. Talking with a counselor can help you gain new perspectives, explore options you never would have thought to consider, and process feelings that are overwhelming you. Making the choice to see a therapist is not a sign of weakness; it is downright courageous and certainly a step toward healing.

If you have never been to counseling before, it can be a bit intimidating at first. You will want to do your research and be sure that you go to a Bible-believing therapist. Between the time you make the appointment and the time it arrives, you will likely try to talk yourself out of going. Don't back out. Be courageous. Counseling might just be a tool that God uses to lead you to the other side. When you arrive for your first appointment, expect some basic paperwork before you begin. You can also expect to be asked the question, "What brings you to counseling?" You may be ready to spill for the next four days, or you may not have any clue where to begin. If you are unsure, I'd like to suggest that you start here: "I need help." This three-word confession will open the door for you to be transparent about the burdens you are carrying. You will be a secret sufferer no more.

I have sat on both sides of the counseling room for many years now. I won't lie; it was difficult to be the client when I first began. I had to fight to keep going back week after week. With the start of therapy, I was reliving everything that I had fought so hard to forget. Everything that was once familiar and comfortable in my life crumbled as I began to deal with the truth of my past. Nothing was normal once I began to share my narrative. Some days I would leave my session so broken I was not sure I would be able to pick myself up off the ground and certainly could not return to work that day. There was even a time when my mentor and her husband showed up at my place late one night unexpectedly, put me in their car, and drove me to their house because they were too scared of me being by myself. For an independent person like myself, that was a hard pill to swallow. They knew I would feel stripped of control; they knew I would be mad; but they loved me enough to do it anyway.

With the onset of counseling, it did get worse before it got better. However, the more I went to counseling, the more I realized how much I had lost in my traumatic experiences, and the more I realized I had lost, the more I was determined to fight to regain it. Soon, I began to look forward to going. I learned more about myself than I ever could have imagined. I credit counseling with partly saving my life. It is worth the time. It is worth the money. Beginning my journey in counseling prepared me for what would come next by processing what had happened previously. And perhaps counseling is a tool that God can use to lead you to the other side too.

"When we choose to believe the lie
that we can make it on our own, we
are robbing the church of one of its
fundamental God-ordained tasks."

8

Daily Homework

One afternoon while I was at work not too long after the coffee shop conversation, I got a text message that read, "Rejoice always. Report 3 rejoicings to me tonight." It came in the form of a command. It was a homework assignment, one I knew she would ask me about that evening. I was at a marketing event for the company I worked for having to engage in conversation with a fake smile plastered across my face with strangers stopping by the booth to learn more about us. I was dying on the inside but forced to be Ms. Public Relations on the outside. I rolled my eyes at first when I read the text thinking, "There really isn't a whole lot to rejoice about today." However, I knew her intent was to help me refocus my racing thoughts. I managed to come up with my three rejoicings and reported them to her, as pathetic as they might have been. Little did I know that would become a daily homework assignment that she would hold me accountable to complete for months. At first, I was rejoicing in being able to keep a meal down, in uninterrupted sleep, and in comfortable shoes as I stood at the booth. And quite honestly, I was struggling to come up with even those. It is so much more natural to identify and dwell on the negative. But as days turned into weeks, the homework assignment became easier. I fought to see God's hand at work in my life. I fought to find hidden treasures throughout each day. The more I fought, three rejoicings became four. Four became twenty. Twenty became fifty.

I think about Philippians 4:4 often. "Rejoice in the Lord always. I will say it again: Rejoice!" No better assignment has ever been given to me than to journal such things. I began to add my own rules to the homework assignment. I wouldn't allow myself to list salvation; that was a given. I wouldn't allow myself to list family; that, for me, was a given. And slowly, over time, my heart began to rejoice as I looked in unexpected places. I began to rejoice in unforeseen phone calls from friends, in words of encouragement sent in an email from someone who had no idea what was going on in my life, and in flannel sheets on a cold night. I rejoiced in phrases from God's word that jumped off the page to me and in being able to sit with my back to folks and remain calm. I rejoiced in a cool breeze, a clean house, and a fingernail polish color that made me smile. I rejoiced in song lyrics that spoke to my heart and in opening my eyes to a new morning with a desire to get out of bed and see the world. It became easier to notice the mysterious hand of God at work. Looking back, I can see that God never left me. Not only did He not leave me, He opened my eyes to how He was quietly orchestrating things around me that had once gone unnoticed. Paul's instruction does not say, "Rejoice when things are going like you want them to go. Rejoice when you feel like it. Rejoice when others around you are rejoicing." He simply said to rejoice. Always.

Choosing to find joy in each day does not mean that we must be silent about our sorrows. Rather, God uses our sorrows to declare a type of rejoicing that we wouldn't be able to proclaim otherwise. Choosing to rejoice doesn't eradicate our sorrows, but it does declare that even in the deepest dark our God is at work orchestrating a triumph beyond our wildest dreams. When we've taken stock of our grief and know the extent of our loss but still choose to declare the goodness of God, we declare to the world that we believe our God is stronger than the storms of this life. We have confidence in a God who is hovering above the storm and know we can find rest under the shadow of His wings. When we look above the storm to gaze upon the Lord, we reach an altitude that alters our attitude. Even if your earthly dreams and hopes have been shattered, our eternal hope will never be shaken.

I can't help but think about one of my favorite stories in the Bible. This story is likely not unfamiliar to you. Jesus and His disciples, leaving the crowd behind, got in a boat to retreat to the other side of the lake. During the night, a fierce storm came, tossing the boat back and forth. Jesus' disciples were terrified, fearing for their lives. I can imagine them looking at one another with a deer-in-the-headlights look wondering what they were going to do. I can just picture them looking down toward their feet when a lightning bolt shot across the sky or cowering with the sound of a monstrous thunderclap. I wonder which one of them had the bright idea to wake up the one passenger on board who was sound asleep. What was their intention in doing so? Did they think that Jesus could really do something about the storm, or were they just saying, "Hey man, you might wanna wake up and enjoy your last moments alive because we're all about to drown." You know the story. Jesus got up, rebuked the wind and the waves, and the waters were instantly stilled. In a second, all was calm. The disciples asked, "Who is this? Even the wind and the waves obey Him."

Aren't you glad that the winds and waves of life obey Christ? There is not a circumstance in your life that God did not allow to be there. There is not a storm that God is unaware exists. But perhaps the reason that this story is among my favorites is because of the very first line. Luke 8:22 records, "One day, Jesus said to His disciples, 'Let's go over to the other side of the lake.'" Mark 4:35 records, "That day when evening came, He said to His disciples, 'Let us go over to the other side.'" Do you see the promise? Jesus told them they would make it to the other side of the lake. Don't you think that Jesus knew what was between them and the other side? He knew a storm would come, but His invitation to His disciples was to go with Him to the other side. Jesus was not surprised by the waves crashing over into the boat. He did not lose faith because of the storm. He was focused on reaching the other side.

Standing on the shore of the Sea of Galilee, the other side is easily visible. When Jesus said to the disciples "Let us go to the other side" if it was a day with clear visibility, they could see the other side. The disciples thought it was going to be a quick, easy trip. Then, of course, the storm kicks up and their faith wavers.

Perhaps you are in the boat. The rain is pelting you on every side. The sky is dark and treacherous. The lightning strikes are overwhelming. You are scared and long for the storm to pass. Remember this: God's promise is that you *will* reach the other side. He is in the boat, fully aware of the storm raging all around you. He knew the storm would come long before it ever did. He hears the longing of your heart for it to end. I just want to encourage you that if you can see the other side, if you can see where God is taking you, if you know what God has promised you, if it's right there but the storm has kicked up and you're right in the middle of the winds and the waves and it seems like Jesus is asleep and your boat is being tossed back and forth by the waves, don't be disheartened. If you've got sight of it, if God has promised you that He's taking you there, then you can know for sure you are on your way no matter how hard times get.

Could He put an end to the waves crashing all around? Could

He put an end to your pain and heartache and suffering? Of course. In an instant. Even the winds and the waves obey Him. But sometimes, in His sovereignty, He chooses not to. That doesn't mean He doesn't love you, even when it does not feel like love. That doesn't mean He has forgotten you, even when it feels like you have been forgotten. God is in the boat, wanting to show you more about Himself so that when you reach the other side, your love for Him is a little deeper and the Gospel shines a little brighter through your life.

Looking back over the experiences that I have had in my life so far, I can see that every significant milestone I have had with the Lord happened in a storm. The moments that I can go back to as a time when I was changed in the presence of the Lord or as an instant when I learned a lesson that I could not have learned otherwise are moments when I was in the midst of suffering. That is why, in the center of the storm, we can rejoice. Habakkuk 3:17-19 says, "Though the fig tree does not bud and there are no grapes on the vines, though the olive crop fails and the fields produce no food, though there are no sheep in the pen and no cattle in the stalls, *yet I will rejoice in the Lord*, I will be joyful in God my Savior. The Sovereign Lord is my strength; He makes my feet like the feet of a deer, He enables me to go on the heights." Rejoice … always. Here's your homework assignment:

1.

2.

3.

"God uses our sorrows to declare a
type of rejoicing that we wouldn't
be able to proclaim otherwise."

9

Do It Scared

As I look back over the seasons of my life, I can easily see times when I have taken some very brave steps all while being downright scared to death. Courage is choosing to jump despite your legs trembling beneath you. Bravery is not the absence of fear. It is choosing to move forward despite the fear. The summer after I graduated college, I boarded an airplane for the Philippines with only a few supplies in a hiker's backpack: a tent, two changes of clothes besides the one on my back, five military meals, a jar of peanut butter, basic toiletries, and my camera. I joined a small team of other college students eager to share the Gospel with those who had never heard it before. The other students worked as an agricultural training team, teaching the local people how to survive off the land, while I served as the photojournalist. Those three months would prove to be some of the most strenuous conditions I have ever endured. I slept in a tent night after night on the hard floor. On my third night in a foreign country, a monsoon came through and blew away one of my two changes of clothes that had been hanging on the clothes line. I washed my clothes by hand with a bar of soap on a large rock next to the river. When it would rain, I would run and grab my shampoo and let the falling waters rinse my hair out, as that was my only "running water." I learned to kill and cook my own chicken and how to harvest rice from the muddy swamplands. I learned that summer what Paul meant when he said in Philippians 4:12, "I have learned the secret of being content in any and every situation, whether well fed or hungry, whether living in plenty or in want."

My small team spent our weekends away from the agricultural fields hiking into a remote village named "Dreamland," only accessible by foot. Dreamland— it's a village ironically named. A handmade pool table served as endless hours of entertainment; electricity had not made its way that far into the mountain; and villagers walked quite a distance down the side of a mountain to retrieve water from the river, which they carried in large plastic buckets on their heads back to their huts. Its people, no more than twenty families in all, were plagued with malaria and malnutrition. Their odds of survival were not good. Their children were dying from the most treatable diseases, but they simply did not know better. Nor did they have knowledge of the God of the universe.

Somehow, the Lord was able to use a few Americans and their translator to begin to turn a hopeless people into those who hoped when it made no sense to hope. The first house we went to belonged to a 75-year-old widow—frail, wrinkled, emotionless. She sat on the floor of her bamboo hut with her knees pulled to her chest. One of my teammates began to share her testimony, and when she pulled out a Bible to read a Scripture passage, the woman froze. Her eyes grew in size as they went from looking into a foreigner's face to the book that was in her hands. It was the first book she had ever seen. While she could not read the words on its pages, she clung to the words that were spoken from it and prayed to receive Christ there in her dusty hut.

As is typically the case when our enemy does not like what we are doing, he began to attack. When we returned to Dreamland the following weekend, we discovered that the leader of the local cult had visited every house that we had, warning them of "the danger" they would be in should they choose to become a Christian. The villagers, who had once been so welcoming and inviting, were cold and callous. They stared as we walked by. They walked away as we approached. With the exception of our new 75-year-old friend, they shunned us.

We decided to return a day early the next weekend, completely unannounced, and simply pray for a movement of God throughout that village. We hiked for hours into the heart of the village in that hot Filipino summer sun. We weren't sure what to expect when we arrived but sensed that God's hand was moving among those people. One by one, they made their way to the group of shade trees we were praying under. I can remember the feel of the sweat pouring down my face after hours of hiking in the dead of summer in a country close to the equator to reach those people. By the time I got there, I was exhausted. I was hot. I was stinky. My body was worn out and, if I were honest, my spirit was depleted. But God's voice began to whisper to my soul: "Tell them there's another side. Tell them of the hope that can only be found in Me."

I looked up and there among the crowd was the cult leader who had instilled such fear just days earlier. "Can I do this?" I thought. "Can I really stand in the middle of this foreign country and share this message through a translator to a culture I know nothing about?" But as quickly as my fears began to rise, so did my courage. I stood on a tree stump that day and declared the goodness of God. I shared with tears streaming down my face that God is a God of forgiveness and grace and compassion and love to measures we could never fully comprehend. I did it scared. And before long, people from surrounding villages had hiked in to see what was going on and I found myself standing before dozens of people sharing about the God who can lead people from darkness and despair to the other side. The very next day, we saw three new believers baptized in the local river. It had nothing to do with me, but everything to do with people desperate for hope that can only be found in Jesus Christ. When people catch even the smallest glimmer of hope, a quiet confidence is born that can alter the entire course of their life.

That summer was a pivotal point in my walk with the Lord. When living conditions challenge every ounce of patience and you find yourself as far from your comfort zone as humanly possible, you have a decision to make. You either walk away, and say, "It's too hard," or you dig your feet in and say, "My God is able." I landed on U.S. soil after that experience with a new-found courage and a set of experiences that I could always look back on and trace God's faithfulness.

I remember another time when I took a brave step that would not make sense to most. I had been back from the Philippines and working for about a year when I sensed God calling me to pursue a master's degree. Now granted, I've never liked school. Not one day of it. While I excelled academically, it never came easy. I had to work for every achievement I earned. My undergrad degree was in journalism communications and I was working in that field at a job I loved. But I was also working with adolescents at my church and felt like I had encountered situations in walking alongside them that I was unprepared to handle. I knew in my gut that the Lord was telling me to pursue a future in the counseling field. As I began to explore what that might mean, I learned about a degree program in marriage and family therapy at a nearby seminary. Let me stop you right there. This made no sense. None. Not even a little. Nada. In college, I did not even take intro to psychology. And did I mention that I hated academics? Why would I leave a well-paying job that I loved to be indebted to grad school, which I was sure to hate? I had a thousand reasons not to pursue this absurdity. But delayed obedience is not obedience. Swift obedience is what it looks like when our hearts are surrendered to Jesus. I had enough insight into myself to know that if I sensed God was telling me something, I needed to be obedient to pursue it before I stopped long enough to think about it and talk myself out of it.

I called the seminary on a Friday afternoon to inquire about the program. They only accepted twelve students into that program each year and eleven of the spots were already filled. Beyond that, they required a certain score on the Graduate Record Examination (GRE) to be considered for a spot. My next phone call was to the GRE testing center, only to learn that there was only one date the test was being offered in time and it was the following Saturday. I drove to the nearest bookstore and bought a GRE prep guide and became a hermit for the next week practicing math equations I had not seen in years and reciting vocabulary I still haven't used again to this day. That Saturday as I drove to the testing center I prayed, "God if you want me to do this program, this score matters." (As though He didn't know that already!). Trembling, I took the test and got the exact minimum score required to be considered for a spot in the program. I called the school and began classes the following Monday. The whole process was a whirlwind, to say the least. I did it scared. In a matter of two weeks, the whole course of my life changed.

Another brave step I can recall was the first time I was assigned a client whose story was eerily similar to mine. I had walked in her shoes as a survivor of abuse. I shared her slashes that screamed she was fighting to live. I knew with all too familiar clarity the gripping panic associated with certain sounds, names, and smells. But here I was working as a therapist staring at a younger version of myself across the room. It was an act of bravery to listen attentively as she shared the grueling details of her story. Yet, in the same way that others saw value in me in the depths of my valley, I saw value in her. It became a cycle of hope: experience rubbing experience. There is perhaps no greater courage I have expressed than being present and available to her and the dozens who have come since her— even when it caused me to step back into my own trauma. That hasn't made me weak; it's made me real. The rawness of knowing the pain personally and still having the capacity to hold it for another is proof that you can be trembling scared but confidently courageous at the same time.

Then there's the bravery of choosing to share my story for the very first time that day in the coffee shop. Quiet courage. Bravery that says, "This may make things worse before they get better, but I'm going to do it anyway." I'm here to tell you that I've never once regretted taking a brave step. If God is asking you to do something, even a small as reading this book, then muster up whatever tiny ounce of courage you have and walk in obedience, my friend. Facing your past trauma will be the scariest thing you've ever done. It will open up scars you long thought had been healed. It will cause you to question the very essence of your existence. If you don't think you can ... you're right. You can't. But He can through you. The first step in the disciples reaching the other side was to get in the boat. They didn't know how long it would take them to reach the shore on the other side or what would happen in the process, but they got in the boat. What boat is God calling you to step in to? What step of bravery is He asking you to take? Don't delay ... the other side is waiting!

"Swift obedience is what it
looks like when our hearts are
surrendered to Jesus."

10

Replacing the Lies

I remember the humid August morning my phone rang as all eyes were glued to the television screen. I was living in Mississippi and news anchors on every television station were trying to find words for the swirling white mass moving across the Gulf of Mexico headed toward land. The call was to head to Gulfport, Mississippi to join search-and-rescue crews and ultimately cleanup efforts after Hurricane Katrina devastated the Mississippi and Louisiana coastlines.

When I managed to arrive on location, the scene was horrific. The sights and smells are ones I hope I never experience again. The devastation the storm left in its wake was absolutely heartbreaking. Buildings ripped from their very foundations. Interstate asphalt literally in pieces. Staircases leading to nothing. Homes left standing with holes in the roof where residents had tried to escape as the waters rose. I spent the next month in the heart of the worst-hit areas, walking among the rubble, lifting pieces of debris hoping to find signs of life and hope underneath. I held hands with people who had lost loved ones and everything they owned. I saw broken dreams and crushed hope. And it was in that experience that God taught me a valuable lesson: What we know to be true before a crisis strikes is still true as we stand in the rubble.

We must know the truth before the crisis so that when the crisis comes, we don't crumble under the weight of the debris. 2 Corinthians 1:10 says, "He has delivered us from such a deadly peril, and He will deliver us again. On Him we have set our hope that He will continue to deliver us." Did you catch that? He has delivered us in the past, He delivers us now, and He will continue to deliver us. Our God is a Deliverer. That, my friend, is the truth.

There is not a day that goes by that I still don't fight lies in my head. As I have waded my way through the murky waters of trauma, I have learned to implement a strategy that has been a lifeline for me. It became essential that I learn to recognize lies quickly and counter them with the truth. Fighting the lies has not become easier with more water under the bridge, but I have learned how to recognize lies quickly so I can replace them before they cause too much damage. For me, I know I am in trouble when I begin to ruminate on thoughts, when I open the door for a lie to enter and allow it to make itself at home. That's why I have to choose to believe what I know to be true rather than what I feel to be true. I feel alone. God says I am never alone. I feel fearful. God says I have nothing to fear. I feel defeated. God says in my weakness He is strong. I feel out of control. How can we be out of control when we're in the hands of the One who controls the universe?

The enemy says, "You're a failure." "You deserve condemnation." "You should have been stronger." "You're a burden." "You're damaged goods." "You're too much to handle." "You're a failure." "No one is trustworthy." "No one will ever love the real you." Those are just a few of the ones I hear, but the reality is that when we are able to shut out one lie, the enemy moves forward with another one that can stab a little deeper. That is precisely why it is essential that I know what is true and claim truth even when it doesn't *feel* true. We must immediately replace a lie with the truth.

I'd love to tell you that I have this concept completely figured out, but it is still a daily struggle for me to live out. Just this morning, I felt the lies of enemy as I heard that all too familiar voice whisper, "Do you really have a message worth sharing?" And for a moment, fear crept in. It was the kind of fear that feels like a bowling ball has fallen on your chest and the room is closing in on you. I've been there before— plenty of times— so I knew that the only thing that would hush its voice was shouting the truth.

If I could cup your cheeks in my hands and look straight into your eyes right now, this is what I'd say. Listen to me. God's not mad at you. He's not disappointed! He says you're worthy. Yes, *YOU*. No matter what lies or how many lies you are hearing at this moment, hear this truth: In Him, there is no condemnation. None. Zero. For those of you who feel like you have royally messed up, lift your head. For those who know you've blown it, you're not alone. I have too. And you know what? He still forgives us as far as the east is from the west! His love—and His alone—is unconditional. You are fearfully and wonderfully made. He made you in His image. He will never leave you nor forsake you. He says when you walk through the fire that you will not be burned. Nothing can ever separate you from His love. We can come with our broken pieces, our shattered hearts, our shameful scars, our every failure, and He will pick up the pieces and rebuild a life far better than you can imagine. He will touch your scars and remind you of the grace that has pulled you from the pit. He will lean your head against His chest and rock you back and forth as the tears fall, emptying you to be refilled with His love and His truths.

Don't believe that you're not good enough, that you've been hurt too badly, and that you've gone too far in the wrong direction.

Don't listen to others whose love for you is conditional and who abandon you when you need help the most. Don't listen one more moment to Satan's lies heaping condemnation into your life. We've all messed up. We're all sinners in need of grace. We're all helpless and hopeless without Him. Raise your head. He's wanting to make eye contact with you and wrap you in His arms. He is for you. He is with you. His love is never failing. You are not alone. You are worthy because He who is in you is worthy. He has a specific purpose for your life. He is pursuing you!

Breathe in. Breathe out. Feel the cool air invade your lungs like His love invades our broken lives. No matter what life has thrown at you, no matter what disappointments or heartaches have come your way, God is good and you are loved. Below is a list of truths that I have, at various seasons of my life, posted where I can regularly see them and claim them when the lies of the enemy come. This simple practice is necessary for me because every single day our enemy continues to throw darts of lies my way. What lies are you being told today in the dark that you need to bring into the light with the truth?

- God is my refuge and strength, an ever-present help in trouble. Psalm 46:1-3
- The Lord is my rock, my fortress, my deliverer, my shield, and my stronghold. Psalm 8:2
- God is my hiding place. Psalm 32:7
- God is the strength of my heart and my portion. Psalm 73:26
- With the Lord I find rest. Matthew 11:28-29
- I will be found by God. Jeremiah 29:13
- I am more than a conqueror. Romans 8:37
- No one can snatch me out of His hand. John 10:29
- He will never forsake me. Psalm 9:10

+ His love for me is unending. Isaiah 54:10, Jeremiah 31:3
+ He will never abandon me. Hebrews 13:5, 1 Samuel 12:22
+ God cares about my suffering. Psalm 31:7
+ My name is written on His hand. Isaiah 49:16
+ God does not hold my sin against me. Colossians 2:13-14, Psalm 103:12
+ God has lots of good planned for me. Psalm 40:5
+ He will always be faithful, even when I am not. 2 Timothy 2:13
+ There will be a day that comes that will not contain pain or tears. Revelation 21:4
+ He knows what I need before I even ask. Matthew 6:8
+ He will finish the good work He has started in me. Philippians 1:6
+ Christ has set me free. Galatians 5:1
+ He will lift my head. Psalm 3:3
+ God thinks of me often. Psalm 139:17-18
+ God fights for me. Exodus 14:14
+ He supplies all my needs. 2 Corinthians 9:9
+ I belong to God. Psalm 100:3
+ Nothing can separate me from the love of God. Romans 8:35-39
+ God's plans for me are good. Jeremiah 29:11
+ No one can snatch me from His hand. John 10:28
+ God delights in me. Psalm 18:19
+ I am valuable to God. Matthew 10:28-31

Are you standing among a pile of debris trying to catch your breath? Are you looking around wondering, "How can anything good come from this?" The same things that were true before your crisis wrecked your world are true today. God's Word is Truth, and the Truth will set you free!

"What we know to be true before
a crisis strikes is still true as
we stand in the rubble."

11

Not Alone

Never underestimate the power behind the words, "I am proud of you." Still to this day, when I hear someone voice those words to me, something special happens on the inside. It's a boost of confidence. It's a breath of fresh air. It's the courage I need to keep on going. I can't help but smile. To be weak in the presence of another and for them to be proud of you is like feeling rejuvenated after an intense workout. While you have to convince yourself to get up off the couch to go exercise and may not particularly enjoy the process of burning calories at the time, there is a deep sense of satisfaction when you are done. Every step I took toward reaching the other side was difficult work, but to hear others say "I am proud of you" along the way gave me a deep sense of contentment that was ultimately the motivation I needed to press on. They didn't just wait until I was "better" to express being proud of me either; they were proud of me for each forward step toward healing.

Sometimes life requires us to walk through the wilderness. As much as we hate that, we know it is true. We have all experienced it. Grief hurts. Pain stings. Healing is a strenuous process. There will be seasons when we cannot walk through the valley alone. Sure, there is One who is always with us, One who will never leave us, and One who has experienced the very griefs that are tearing us apart. But we will also need someone in human flesh who can carry hope for us when we have none. We need someone to believe in us when we don't believe in ourselves. We need someone courageous enough to not accept "fine" for an answer when they ask us how we are doing. We need someone who pursues us when all we want to do is isolate ourselves. We need someone to force us to make direct eye contact. We need someone patient enough to repeat over and over and over again as many times as it takes that there is another side and that we will make it to it. We all need our person.

Not too long ago, I was flipping back through some old journals. I found where I had written, "After church tonight, she got right up beside me and stared straight into my eyes. I looked back at her and she said, 'I just needed to know if you could do it. You can look away, but I just needed to know you could look at me.'" I chuckled when I read that because what she was saying was, "I know you're not doing well, but I need to know that you are not pushing me away. I need to know that you know I am for you, I am with you, and I love you."

There is a crazy irony that takes place in life. God created us to be in relationships with other people. He placed us in families. He ordained marriages. His word talks about mentors and teachers and friends. It's not a shock that God did not intend for us to live in isolation. The irony, however, is that it is people who hurt us and also people who help us heal. Healing begins in the context of a safe relationship, yet when we've been hurt by people, relationship is the last thing we want. Galatians 6:2 tells us to carry each other's burdens. Oftentimes, we read that as a command to help those around us—but consider the reverse for a moment. If you are the one who needs help carrying your burdens, you must be willing to let others help you carry them. When you have been wounded by people, allowing others in can be a terrifying thought. But the reality is that you need those around you who believe in you and who can help you connect the dots to understand that you are not crazy as you experience what seems to be a thousand different emotions.

It is so easy to want to push your grief under the rug and pretend it doesn't exist. You will want to convince yourself that you have dealt with the pain and moved on long before you know you have. You will tell yourself that your emotions are silly and that you need to get over it. If you are like me, you will tell yourself that you are making a bigger deal out of this than necessary. You will want to minimize, deny, or discount your suffering. You will tell yourself, "At least it didn't kill me," when in fact you feel dead. It is critical to have someone walking through the valley with you who will refuse to let you deny the reality that you are grieving. As you feel angry, depressed, scared, and chaotic, you need someone reminding you that all of those feelings are normal. You are not crazy. The pain is real. There is another side.

Another irony in all of this is that, although we need each other, no one can fully understand what you are going through. The one who did not experience the pain firsthand can never fully understand how the sufferer feels, while the one who did can never fully communicate it in a way that others could entirely comprehend. Many times, words are insufficient to convey an experience. However, words are necessary in the healing process. Only when we are able to put words to our experiences can we find relief from trauma. It meant the world to me when I found a safe person who was willing to walk through the valley with me. She would often say, "We're in this together. It's us now." I would look at her and tear up every time, knowing that she meant it with all her heart. Slowly, the Lord began to show me more safe people to become a net under me to catch me when I'd fall. And in time, He made me a safe person for others. Safe people are those who love you even when they know everything about you, who challenge you by asking the tough questions most are scared to ask, and who see you consistently enough to know how you are really doing. Yes, it is people who scar us, but it is also people who help lead us to the other side. Allow others to help you. Will they disappoint you? Most likely, because people are fallible, but the risk is worth it. You were never meant to walk this journey alone.

"Healing begins in the context of a safe relationship, yet when we've been hurt by people, relationship is the last thing we want."

12

The Upside of Setbacks

Today has been filled with my daughter's four-year-old crisis. Her stuffed grey "Flopsy" bunny went missing. We looked under furniture. We looked in every closet. We looked in the car. We looked high and low but had no luck in locating her favored plush toy. I was about out of patience when she grabbed me by the shoulder, looked me in the eyes and said, "Never give up, Mommy. Keep going." *Never give up.* Once again, my preschooler reminded me of an invaluable life lesson.

The lesson to never give up is one I've had to learn on my own journey to healing. There have been bends in the road that seemingly detoured me from the destination of healing. But if I had given up when I could no longer see the goal, I'd have never seen just how perfectly God was orchestrating the road to freedom. It had been more than five years since I had struggled with self-harm, a practice that often accompanies those who have experienced trauma. I couldn't believe I had fallen back into the trap that I had overcome for so long. I had gone years without so much as a thought of harming myself, and now the shame was too intense to pick myself up off the floor. I felt like a complete failure, a total fraud, a disappointment. How could I really start back at *zero* after all this time? Did this mean that all my healing up to that point was in vain? It was a chest-crushing feeling to face the fact that I still had demons in an area I had fought so hard for victory.

For me, it works like a cycle. I first cut because I was mad at my arms for not protecting me. And then I cut to punish myself because I had cut. And then I cut because I should have been stronger than to turn to cutting in the first place. And before long, an addiction was born that had the potential to destroy me.

The first time I felt the cold metal slice against my forearm, I felt nothing. I longed to feel something, anything. I had no desire to die; rather, I was fighting with everything in me to live. The shallow sliver was enough for red to run, and the red was a sign to myself that I was indeed still alive. The pain I was feeling had not swallowed me up. Although my heart was pounding, and my chest felt like it was caving in, I had proof that I was indeed alive.

I learned a long time ago not to say that I would never struggle with something because that would be the very thing Satan could use to trap me. I have a dear friend who works at a Methadone clinic who regularly says, "We are all one car accident away from being there." I've seen far too many clients who say they would never struggle with bulimia who now find themselves sprawled out on the bathroom floor night after night. I've had several friends who once told me they would never turn to drugs who now find themselves sitting on folding chairs in recovery centers. And I would have told you that I'd never struggle with self-harm and will now always declare myself a recovering addict.

"Never give up, Mommy." My daughter's words play on repeat in my head. I remember the slow climb out of addiction. Every single day that I chose not to hurt my body was a victory. I'd get to three, and then four, and then back to zero. I'd go again.

One, two, three, four, five, six, zero. And eventually the number of days grew into months and months grew into years. I'd love to tie my story up with a pretty bow on top and report a "happily ever after" ending, but I vowed to be fully authentic. Even after years, I relapsed. I'm not sure an addiction ever fully goes away, but I have never given up. The truth is that we are not defined by our relapses but rather our decision to stay in recovery despite them. Relapse is a part of recovery; it is not failure. Setbacks force us to stop, regroup, and make a decision as to whether we are going to get back up and try again or not. In the moment of a setback, we have a defining decision to make. We can give up and resign ourselves to being trapped in poor coping mechanisms. Or, we can muster whatever courage we have, draw a line in the sand and declare, "I'm forging on!"

I sat across from my therapist friend after that relapse, pulled up my sleeve, and lay my arm exposed to the shame and ridicule I just knew was coming. But it never came. At the very least, I deserved a "What in the world were you thinking?" but that didn't come either. Instead, she bravely embraced the very parts of me that repulsed me the most and said, "Even that doesn't scare me off." I began to unravel the details of what I had done, and she looked at me with nonjudgmental eyes. When my sharing was over, I waited for the response I was sure would give me the punishment I deserved.

"Let me tell you again how proud I am of your bravery."

Hold on. Wait a minute. Excuse me?

"Proud of this?" I asked, extending my own Scarlet Letter.

"I am proud of your willingness through all this to be transparent with me."

It was another one of those moments I will never forget, where I was fully known and fully loved. I was exposed, and it changed nothing. I don't have all the answers when it comes to navigating the waters of trauma, but I do have my own personal experiences of knowing what certain struggles feel like, and I'm just crazy enough to believe that perhaps I'm not the only one who has had them. While I don't claim to have all the answers, there is something I know with absolute certainty: to be known is to be loved, and to be loved is to be known. Otherwise, what's the point in doing either one of them in the first place? To be fully known, received, accepted, and loved by another in all our mess is the very picture of the Gospel.

God saw our mess and He chose to leave the royalty of heaven and come down into it. Jesus knows us intimately. He knows the deep crevices that we work so hard to cover up. He sees the pain that is so dark we can't even utter it. He grabs hold of our most shame-filled moments and says, "Even that doesn't scare me off." This, my friend, is what I've learned through my own experiences. This is the Gospel. This is the true story of a God who sees, who cares, and who feels alongside of us. I haven't grown to love the Lord from my mountaintop experiences, although those moments give me the refreshment that I need to journey on. No, I've come to know Him in the valley. I fell in love with Him when He took hold of me at my lowest and never let go. I learned about true Love when I was exposed, and it changed nothing.

He gave His life for *me*— a sinner, an outcast, a disappointment, a failure. Were it not for grace, my identity would be that of the mistakes I have made that carry the most shame for me. But because of grace, I am chosen, wanted, redeemed, worthy, enough, forgiven, and set free. There is not a single thing that I can do to make Him love me any more or any less than He does right now. I cannot earn His love and I cannot lose it. It is a gift, freely given. I can stumble without fear that a single ounce of God's love for me will change. When God looked down and saw my broken state, He embraced it. He met me in the mess. He found me in my filth.

Maybe that's why Jesus came the way He did. Maybe that's why He was born in a humble manger in a filthy barn. Maybe Jesus doesn't come only to the wealthy, to those who have it all together. Maybe Jesus comes to the unworthy, the unclean, those who don't have it together, those who are hurting. Maybe it has something to do with what the angel said that holy night: "Fear not!" Fear not … God has not forgotten about us. Fear not … God keeps His promises. Fear not … God loves us just as we are. He knows everything about us, even the parts we try to keep a secret, and loves us anyway. How can we quit when our setbacks are matched with that kind of love?

"The truth is that we are not defined
by our relapses but rather our decision
to stay in recovery despite them."

13

The Real Me

I have been involved in theater for many years. My interest in stage life began in high school. It really accelerated in college when I toured with a traveling drama troupe. After that, I spent more than a decade directing a youth drama team. I love everything about theater, whether I'm on stage, backstage, or directing what's happening on stage. There is something magical that happens when you are involved in the world of live theater.

I remember the thrill of performance nights. The backstage crew frantically searched for a misplaced prop. The soundman struggled to cue the music at the appropriate time. The director whispered, "Break a leg!" as the star of the show headed for centerstage. We raced backstage, changed costumes, and returned to the spotlight, hoping we remembered all of our lines. As our adrenaline rushed under the beaming lights above, the audience was mesmerized with our ability to bring a story to life. But eventually everything must come to an end.

We took our final bow. The audience gave one last standing ovation. The final curtain closed. I remember one particular night after the final performance of a show series. I sat on the edge of the stage watching the last of the crowd exit the theater. I slowly gazed around at the empty seats, the stage set and the spotlight that no longer shone down on me as it had when I emptied myself and took on another character. I spent hours of preparation creating and perfecting my role. I learned to walk, talk, and eat like my character. I practiced laughing and crying like my character would until I became that character. But when the curtain closed and the last audience member went home, I somehow had to find my original identity again. I took the costume off, but not the character. It is hard to let go of a person you have grown to love.

People who have never experienced the rush that comes with stage life do not understand this love. It is as if they cannot comprehend truly becoming another person. Sure, they enjoy watching other people on stage, but until they have been up there themselves, it is a mere spectacle. Or is it? How many times do we pretend to be someone we are not in real life? How many times do we have a smile painted on our faces when our heart is breaking on the inside? How many times do we fool even ourselves by what we put on the outside?

I have been on both sides of the curtain. I love to watch a play unfold from a chair in the audience. Through watching, I can eavesdrop on someone else's life. But I also know there is more behind the actress than makeup and a costume. One role I vividly remember playing was the part of a teenage drug addict. I played the role of Jan, a high school girl involved with the party crowd. Each night before the show, I would put on a fitted red shirt and black leather jacket. I applied scarlet lipstick, midnight blue eye shadow and teased my hair. Changing my appearance was the first step to becoming Jan.

Looks alone, however, did not make the character. Once the curtain opened and the stage lights lit up, I mentally became a teenage drug addict. After the show, people would approach me asking, "How can you just cry on cue?" or "How do you do that so realistically?" My response was easy: "I didn't; Jan did."

I also remember those unforgettable moments on stage when improvisation skills became my best friend. An actor is not tested until something unexpected happens—someone forgets a line, a prop is missing, the curtain does not close at the end of a scene, a technical aspect goes wrong, or something else unpredictable happens. I still laugh today about ways in which I have used impromptu lines to compensate for mishaps on stage.

My senior year of high school I played the role of Maureen, a psychologist in a mental institution for children, in a play called "David and Lisa." In the middle of the scene, the table my students were seated around collapsed on top of all of them, which wasn't supposed to happen. The character of David had a fear of anyone touching him, so when I went to pick up the table, he screamed and jerked away from me. I then began to console him, and we carried on a five-minute conversation about why he did not need to be afraid of people coming close to him. The audience had no idea that the table falling was an accident. They just assumed we made it collapse in order to have that conversation. As actors, we had become Maureen and David and were able to know how to respond to the unexpected incident.

An actor's goal in learning to become another person is to somehow relate to a spectator watching the show. When an actor completely steps outside of himself and takes on a different personality, the audience members can usually see characteristics of themselves in his performance. Despite all of the preparation it takes to make this happen and the excitement that comes when it is achieved, the show has to end. The audience leaves having evaluated themselves in some small way, but the actor is left to put to death his character. When that final curtain closes, the house lights come on and the cast takes its final bow, the character becomes a mere shadow following the actor until he steps out of the limelight.

A performer's job is martyrdom. Memorize. Block. Rehearse. Practice. Become. When the show ends, however, it is then time to annihilate what they have worked so hard to become. A piece of the actor leaves with each character every time the final curtain closes. The set is taken down. The props are placed in a storage closet for use in future performances. That night that I gazed one last time around the auditorium and made my way to the exit door, a tear quietly rolling down my cheek. I flipped the last light switch off and waved goodbye to another show, another character, another piece of myself.

It's no different on the stage of life. We work so hard to be the character we want to be rather than the person we know we are. Somewhere along the way, we've all learned it. Someone has taught each one of us how to "put on the mask," if you will— how to pretend that we're okay when we're really not. You don't have to think too hard to know that this is true. "Good morning. How are you today?" is almost always followed with, "I'm fine, thanks." It's like if we're not fine, the socially acceptable thing to do is to pretend we are anyway. Why is that? We've painted on the smiles and put up walls to hide our weaknesses, even inside our own church. Don't get me wrong, I can play the game with the best of them. But ... if we're going to build up the body of Christ, we've got to remove the masks.

We think that if we can convince everyone else that we are strong and fearless, we might actually believe it too. On the outside, we shine. But on the inside, we are all scarred, bruised, and broken. Truth is, if we'd all remove our masks, we'd be surprised by how similar we look. We've all been broken. If we keep hiding our pain from each other, how will the world ever know there is a God who loves the brokenhearted? Authenticity is a magnet for others to let down their guard and find healing as well.

When we take off the masks that hide us from one another, maybe we'll find we're not so alone. And maybe, just maybe, we'll remember that we serve a God whose own scars, bruises, and brokenness became our salvation. If I didn't know brokenness, then how could I know wholeness? If I hadn't experienced sorrow, how could I ever appreciate joy? And if I never acknowledged the raging storms I had survived, how would I ever have known the safety and peace of the other side?

Do you ever find yourself trying to look a certain part? I do! I can remember when I finally felt the burden of my sorrow lift. I wasn't sure who I was anymore. For so long, I had carried such intense heartache, yet very few knew. I memorized, blocked, and rehearsed until I became what those in the audience of my life perceived as a content and happy person. When the Lord delivered me from the pit, I had to put that character to death. I had to annihilate what I had worked so hard to become, because ultimate freedom comes when we are completely real. I was no longer the "be strong and hold it all together" girl. I could be me— broken and whole at the same time, scarred but healed. I was left to discover my original identity—the identity that God intended for me to have, the identity I am given as a child of His. Sometimes we are in such a desolate place for so long that we don't even remember who we were before we got there. When Jesus calms the winds and the waves around us, we often reach the other side as someone different than the person who left the shore.

"If we keep hiding our pain from each other, how will the world ever know that there is a God who loves the brokenhearted?"

14

Facing Our Giants

My favorite Bible story is found in 1 Samuel 17. This chapter records the familiar story of David and Goliath: a scrawny boy versus a stout, nine-foot giant. I believe this story has a lot to share with us about reaching the other side. David had just come to the battlefield to bring his brothers some nourishment when he heard the hecklings of Goliath. Verse 26 records, "David asks, 'For who is this uncircumcised Philistine that he should taunt the armies of the living God?'" I love that David's immediate response to Goliath's threats was to imply, "Does this guy not realize who he's messing with?" Who is Satan to taunt a child of the living God? Why do we, like the Israelite army, so often stand back paralyzed by fear when obstacles come at us? Why are we not like David, who was willing to fight believing he would win because he knew he had God on his side?

In verse 37, David then declares, "The Lord who delivered me from the paw of the lion and from the paw of the bear, He will deliver me from the hand of the Philistine." David looked back on God's past faithfulness to fortify his faith for this fight. After the hundreds of clients I have worked with, I still have some who come into my office and their stories are so eerily familiar to my own that I wonder, "Can I really do this? Can I walk them through the details of their pain without being swallowed back up in it myself?" But then I remember that God orchestrated all of the details of securing me the last spot in my postgraduate program for such a time as this. He picked me up off the kitchen floor that night and has brought me this far for a purpose. When we are able to look back and see the storms of life that God has brought us through, we find an incredible amount of courage to conquer the next giant we are facing.

Preparing to fight Goliath, David then tries on King Saul's majestic armor. Even though it was the best of the best, it didn't work because he was not accustomed to it. Quite simply, it didn't fit. We don't need fancy tools to fight our enemies. We don't have to concoct regal solutions to find bravery to head toward enemy lines. We need to use the tools we are accustomed to already, and the more we use them, the more comfortable we will be with them and the more powerful they will be. So what weapons do I have? His power in me. The shield of faith. The helmet of salvation. The breastplate of righteousness. The belt of truth. Feet fitted with the readiness of the Gospel of peace. The sword of His word that is alive and active. When we fight for the Lord with the armor we are accustomed to, we will not be defeated. In victory, His name is made known, and that is the point of every battle and every breath we take!

When the Philistines saw that their champion was dead, they fled. The army that had stood tall behind their towering hero turned their backs and ran in defeat. Just moments earlier, their confidence was soaring. On the contrary, the Israelites who had been trembling just moments earlier discovered a newfound confidence after they tasted victory. When we defeat the enemy in one area, that victory helps us beat him in other areas as well. The Bible records that when Goliath fell, the men of Israel and Judah arose, shouted, and pursued their enemy. Because of David's courage to step into dangerous territory, the entire Israelite army now had the confidence to charge the enemy. When others see us fight and win, it gives them courage to join us in the battle, where before they were paralyzed by fear.

My courage to fight the battle before me equals victory. My victory then gives others the courage to fight their battles. Others having courage to fight their battles equals their victory. And my victory plus their victory equals Satan's defeat! You see, God didn't make us to be Goliaths. He made us to be Davids who conquer Goliaths. He's not asking us to muster up more of our strength as we head into enemy territory; He's asking us only to rely on His strength. He is our secret weapon.

In Numbers 14, the Israelites allowed the fear of the fight to steal their victory. God had promised them the land, but they were too scared of the giants that had to be conquered in order to obtain it. Because of that, they wasted their life. I do not want to walk around in the wilderness for forty years like the Israelites and die there because I was afraid of the giants that had to be fought. My promised land is worth the effort! So let me ask you this: What are your giants? Are you going to wander in the wilderness because you are too afraid to face them, or are you going to run toward the battle line with a familiar weapon in your hand, knowing that victory is yours if you're willing to fight?

"God didn't make us to be
Goliaths. He made us to be Davids
who conquer Goliaths."

15

The Supernatural Work
of Forgiveness

One of the hardest giants I have ever had to face is forgiveness. I'm guessing for some of you just reading the word "forgiveness" brings up some uneasiness inside. It did for me for the longest time. Forgiveness seems like an impossible feat, a daunting uphill battle to say the least. Forgiveness implies that the other person is off the hook, that what happened to us is okay, and some of us can't stomach the thought of accepting that. We don't have to, because those things are not true. Let me go ahead and take the fear out of this subject matter: forgiveness is a divine act of God. I cannot do it; you cannot do it; but God can do it through us. Let that bring you freedom because the act of forgiving someone is supernatural, and we cannot do it in our own power.

When we have been hurt deeply, it is so hard to let go of bitterness and resentment because our natural tendency is to stay cold in order to protect ourselves. When we have been profoundly wounded, our innate response is to build walls around our heart to protect it from being broken again and to keep everyone at arm's length to have control over whether we will be hurt again. But it's no surprise that the only person who suffers from living behind impenetrable walls is the one trapped inside. The person who suffers most from unforgiveness is the one who harbors it. An unforgiving spirit hinders our relationship with God, the very source of strength we need to heal and move forward.

I remember the night I wrestled with God and finally asked Him to help me forgive my perpetrator. I was sitting in church preparing to partake in communion. My eyes were fixed on the red liquid in a little transparent cup I embraced between my fingers. It was a symbol of the blood of Jesus, a representation that He loved me so much He was willing to die for my sins. I could not help but become queasy when I slowly brought it up toward my lips. I sensed in my spirit that He was asking me to allow Him to change my heart about that person. I held that drop of Jesus' blood in my hand. He told His children to drink of His blood as a remembrance of the appalling day when His body was jolted into place upon that unrelenting cross. This gift of life, given to me because of His death, was given freely. I swallowed hard as the sting of His costly blood trickled down my throat. I looked down at the empty cup, amazed that His blood that spilt years ago on that cruel cross made me whiter than snow. All of the anguish and the agony that Jesus endured set me free from bondage.

"Do this in remembrance of me," He said. How could I *not* remember? I am the one who has shouted insults at Him. I am the one who has spit in the face of the Savior. I am the one whose sin cost Him His is very life. But His grace reached beyond my sin. I struck; He forgave. I scoffed; He forgave. I sin; He still forgives.

A tear trickled down my cheek that night as the reality of my own evil heart became so clear. I have been bought with a price. He took my place. Jesus died once for all men, for all sin, mine included. He bridged the gap between this despicable sinner and the immaculate, holy, and perfect God. I celebrated that night with the Lord 's Supper. It was when I looked in the mirror and saw my own filth that I knew I needed to forgive those who had wronged me.

Forgiveness happens in an instant, yet forgiveness takes time. Forgiveness is a decision in the mind to let something go. That choice happens instantly when the decision to do so is made in the mind. However, the process of seeing that carried out is a lengthy, sometimes lifelong, process. While we make up our minds that we will forgive someone for something they have done to us, forgiveness is a matter of the heart, and only God can change the heart. Transformation is a process. While we outwardly make the moment-by-moment decision to walk in forgiveness, God is doing His supernatural work of changing our hearts on the inside.

In all honesty, I have had much more difficulty forgiving myself through the years than I have anyone else. I am, by far, my worst critic. My expectations of myself far exceed any expectations I could place on another. My own self-condemnation is one of my fiercest enemies. But this is the Gospel: forgiveness isn't something I can give myself or anyone else. It is something He purchased for us all. It is an act of grace, His unmerited favor poured out on us because He loves us. We must accept it. If we don't, we are saying that the cross was not enough. We must open our hands and receive the gift of mercy. If we cannot apply forgiveness to ourselves personally, how can we ever apply it to anyone who has wronged us? If we cannot accept that we are fully forgiven because of Christ's work on the cross, then we are just holding a pretty package with a big bow on top refusing to open it.

I fully believe that when we are able to forgive ourselves because we recognize that God has forgiven us then we can start to process forgiveness as it relates to other people. His forgiveness sets the bar for our daily interactions with others. In 1 Corinthians 3, Paul uses the metaphor of farming. There are certain things the farmer must do— plow, plant, fertilize, irrigate, cultivate, and harvest. But only God makes things grow, and He alone controls the weather. All He asks is that we open our hands, ask Him to do the work that only He can do, and watch Him do so.

"Forgiveness isn't something I can give myself or anyone else. It is something He purchased for us all."

16

Cycle of Hope

I've learned something in my own journey to the other side. The bravest thing I can do is to be real enough to say that I'm broken and scared but still trust that I am loved and held and used for the good of others in my broken and scared state. We don't have to wait until we feel like we have it all together to help others in their time of need. I love watching broken people walk alongside other broken people. It's true that those who have experienced utter shattering are the ones most equipped to be the healing force in another's brokenness. Our realness is what they need. Our raw and heartbreaking pain opens the window for the fresh air of authenticity to come in and be felt. Our doubts, our questions, and our confusion is the very clarity someone else needs to know they are not alone. It's a cycle of hope, and hope is the deadliest poison to the one who roams the earth seeking to destroy and devour.

Perhaps it's in the broken places with broken people that we are most near the heart of Christ. It's through our cracked places that we are able to receive the healing balm and know the steadfast love of a God who sees. There is no crevice too deep, no desert too desolate, that the love of God cannot reach. Is it conceivable to think that the deepest wounds shine the brightest spotlight on the unwavering love of our heavenly Father? We can be agents of hope and healing precisely where we have known the most brokenness.

Psalm 103:2-4 says, "Praise the LORD, my soul, and forget not all his benefits—who forgives all your sins and heals all your diseases, who redeems your life from the pit and crowns you with love and compassion." Those whose lives have been redeemed from the pit can't help but have compassion for others because they remember all too well the depths from which they've been saved. Those who know earth-shattering horrors can speak the most life into those who have lost their voice. Those who can't possibly sugarcoat the feelings associated with trauma are the very ones who are believable as they extend the message of hope.

Just this morning, I was reminded of this very message. My daughter proudly brought me her latest artwork to hang on the refrigerator. It was a purple heart she had drawn and filled with stickers. However, she had placed a sticker on the paper and then decided she wanted to reposition it. In doing so, she ripped the heart before finding the sticker its new location. But to her, it didn't matter. She had a beautiful heart she wanted to mount in the center of the refrigerator.

In the process of trying to display it, she dropped a magnet between the side of the fridge and the edge of the counter. She looked at me with her piercing blue eyes and said, "We've just got to reach in the dark to help it out." *We've just got to reach in the dark to help it out.* It took my breath away. I blinked and wrapped my arms around her. You're right, wise child. When we find ourselves in the darkest night, we reach out for the hope that can only be found in Jesus. We may not see the light, we may not feel his goodness, but we reach knowing that He will take hold of us and lead us to the other side. And when we find ourselves in the peace of the other side, we reach back, and grab hold of those grasping for help. I reached beside the refrigerator and picked up the magnet. I handed it to the innocent child who used it to display the heart she had made, a heart with a small tear at the top.

Why have we believed the lie for so long that we must have it all together before we can help someone else? Wasn't it Jesus' very stripes and scars that made us whole? Wasn't it His death that gave us life? Perhaps our greatest purpose can be found in the exact place of our deepest sorrow. Maybe the most painful wounds birth the most authentic beauty. Maybe it's in the pieces of our story that we never would have chosen that God can use us the most to minister to someone else.

I often find myself listening to someone sharing with me about the pieces of their story wishing so badly that I had magic words to make it all better. I find myself desiring a handful of fairy dust that I could sprinkle that would instantly turn their despair into delight. But I don't have a quick fix, and neither do you. What we do have is the beauty of the Gospel, which says that beauty rises from ashes. It says that death gives way to life. Sometimes— perhaps all of the time—the greatest gift we can give to someone in a crisis is simply to be present with them in their pain. We can be there in the midst of their outrage, their shame, their frailty, their humiliation, their disappointments, their shame, and their doubts and say, "Even that doesn't scare me off. I'm not going anywhere. I'm here. You are not alone."

There are too many individuals suffering silently in our pews, in our neighborhoods, and in our workplaces. Those of us who have tasted the other side must turn around and throw a lifeline to them. Our redemption can be the greatest form of hope to those who are gasping for air. In Psalm 118:17, David penned, "I will not die but live, and will proclaim what the Lord has done." When we have survived horrors that could have killed us, how can we not proclaim how God delivered us? When we have been set free, when we have tasted the other side, when we know the hope that can only come from our Redeemer, we can lock arms and partner with someone else who is walking through their own brokenness. Sometimes, God redeems our stories by surrounding us with others who need to hear about our past, so it doesn't become their future. Only a God who used death to bring life can use our brokenness to bring wholeness to others.

"We can be agents of hope and healing precisely where we have known the most brokenness."

17

In the Middle

None of us would disagree that the other side is a better place to be, but what about the journey *to* the other side? Is it possible that from our perspective on the shore that all we focus on is the opposite shoreline instead of the countless treasures to be gained in the waters between? The deep valleys that we must pass through are the very places where God meets us. The darkest places are where we experience Him most intimately.

I remember a Sunday evening sitting in church when I read Psalm 84:5-7 for the first time. "Blessed are those whose strength is in you, whose hearts are set on pilgrimage. As they pass through the Valley of Baka, they make it a place of springs; the autumn rains also cover it with pools. They go from strength to strength, till each appears before God in Zion." I was unfamiliar with the term "Baka." I began to dig a little deeper. "Baka" means adversity. I was in Baka, in a time of adversity, when I first read this. And since then, I have had my share of seasons of difficulty. The Bible is clear that as long as we are living on this side of eternity, life will be accompanied by adversity. Maybe as you read this, you are there too. Maybe your pain is so private that no one knows you are hurting. Maybe you feel trapped. Our adversities may have different circumstances, different hurts, different fears, different layers, but it is very much the same valley.

The literal Valley of Baka is thousands of miles away in a land that most of us have never traveled. The spiritual Valley of Baka, however, is very familiar. Imagine yourself standing in a desolate place. It is dry and barren. Isolated. The heat of the valley drains the weary travelers. Hope is waning and despair quietly takes its place. No one wishes for Baka, but it is necessary to walk through it to get to the other side.

On the other side is what I needed, what I had been promised, so I set my heart on the journey. But, as is so common, my strength began to fail. Hope was disappearing. Some days I felt confident and filled with strength, and other days I wondered how I would ever make it through. I was often dry. Thirsty. Desolate. Sometimes, there seemed to be no end in sight. Despair set in.

"I wonder if I'll die here?" I thought. "Where has my strength gone?"

In utter desperation and with nowhere else to go, I cried out to God. I wept. My tears mirrored the agony of my heart. But again and again and again, I took a deep breath, set my heart on the journey, and determined to cling to Jesus with all my might. Clinging looks like praising God in the midst of the storm. It looks like believing Him when all our senses contradict what we know to be true. It looks like trusting Him regardless of our circumstances. Quitting in the Valley of Adversity was not an option for me. I fixed my mind on the Goal. I focused my eyes on Truth. He was my strength. He sustained me.

Sometimes I find myself back in the Valley of Baka, but He is always with me. Each time I feel I can't go on and am thirsting to the point of death, He provides nourishment from the springs. He is the God who sees my hurt, frustration, and pain. He knows the valley well. I cannot turn from Baka, for my promise is that I am never alone. My circumstances don't always change. This is Baka, the place of Adversity, where weeping and anguish accompany us until we reach the end of our pilgrimage. But God is here! He holds me when I cry. He wipes the tears. He comforts me when I am lonely. He replaces despair with His presence.

When we reach the end of the Valley of Baka, we will not be defeated. We will be stronger, for we will have learned true strength. We don't grow strong when everything is easy. We don't become brave when walking through certainty. Our greatest qualities are birthed during the dark days. Our resilience is built during the trials of this life. And here is the sweetest treasure of all: we never journey alone. He walks with us, always. Sometimes He is quiet, and we can't hear Him. In those moments, our desire for Him grows more intense as we recognize our desperate need for help. When He speaks, we know that He is the Good Shepherd, leading us lovingly to wide open spaces.

The journey is not a place of rest. Very few giant steps are taken. Rather, this is a journey of one foot in front of the other for as long as it takes to reach the other side. Weariness is a likely guarantee. That is the very reason He says, "Come to Me all of you who are weary, and I will give you rest." This journey is one small step at a time, one act of trust after another, one test of dependence after another.

For those of you experiencing some of life's greatest suffering, I wish that I could give you some perfect formula for reaching a place of freedom, but I can't. I only know that the way out is to deal with all the very things you want to run and hide from. I know, too, that God's word is Truth, and the Truth will set you free. I know that God loves us—unconditionally, madly, eternally. He is the Wide-Open Space on the other side. He is waiting for you there. And when you arrive, you will rest, you will rejoice, and you will see the journey altogether differently from the other side.

"Our greatest qualities are
birthed during the dark days.

Final Thoughts

I don't want to be known for my story; I want to be known for the Author of my story. Anything good that has come out of my story is because of the Author and Finisher of my faith, who gives peace in the broken pieces and gifts in the wilderness. I have scars—some visible, some buried deep within. And since scars tell stories, I have stories—friends that have betrayed, jobs that were lost, dreams that were shattered. I am a victim of sexual abuse. I am divorced. I am a single mom. But I don't want to be known by any of those things; they don't define me. I wear their scars because they are pieces of my story, but they are only pages in a big book that God is writing. I don't want to be known as a victim or a divorcee or any other label that comes from something that has happened to me. I want God to be known as the One who put the broken pieces back together in a more beautiful way than I ever could have. I want Him to be seen in the details of my healing. Lord Jesus, may your testimony in me be "God heals."

I can't believe I'm about to say this, but I am so glad there was a time in my life when my world fell apart and the only thing I had left was my faith. My faith was tested like never before, and it stood the test. Once again, I hear Peter shouting in 1 Peter chapter 1: "Hold on! This trial is just showing off your faith! You're gonna make it!" I didn't necessarily come out on the other side with answers to all my questions, but I learned on such a heart level that God is good and that God is faithful, and that is enough. Knowing those two things answers any question I might have. I know what it is like to have to wait on the Lord. I know what the pit looks like. For me, it was laying on the kitchen floor with tears streaming down my face asking, "Will you remind me one more time that there is another side?" I know the moment God heard my cry and responded. I know a lot about mud and mire, but I also know the Rock.

I want to shout from the rooftops about what God has done in my life. Many will see and put their trust in the Lord, and my prayer is that at least one does so because of my experiences. I wish I could tell you that I'm confident that I'll never again have to ask, "Am I going to make it to the other side?" The truth is that in my flesh I know I will likely face trials and circumstances that test my faith all over again. There will be good days and bad. There will be days when I feel like I'm living through heartache in isolation and days when I am overwhelmed by the support system God provides. There will be days when I stand confidently on a firm foundation, and days when I shout, "O my God, do not delay!" There will be moments when temptations to believe the lies are overwhelmingly powerful. But, having tasted the other side before, I know with all my heart that the battle is worth fighting.

Jesus set me free on the cross not just for salvation, but for freedom. I have learned that everything broken doesn't have to be completely fixed for me to be completely okay. I can be scared and brave and broken and whole and weak and strong at the same time. I can be hurt but don't have to live hurt. I can be broken but don't have to live broken. It's not that I'm not... it's that I'm also! I may be wounded, but I am also held by the God of the universe who sees and knows and cares and cries tears alongside me. I may be battered, but I am also a daughter of the Most High God, the God who restores what the locusts have eaten. I may have been forgotten by some, but I am also loved beyond comprehension by a God who would send His very Son to die in order that I might live. My God holds me together in my brokenness, so that even when I am broken I am completely whole. My friend, He will do the same for you.

"I don't want to be known for my story; I want to be known for the Author of my story."

Printed in the United States
By Bookmasters